SUPERSTITIONS

Brimming with creative inspiration, how-to projects, and useful information to enrich your everyday life, Quarto Knows is a favorite destination for those pursuing their interests and passions. Visit our site and dig deeper with our books into your area of interest: Quarto Creates, Quarto Cooks, Quarto Homes, Quarto Lives, Quarto Drives, Quarto Explores, Quarto Gifts, or Quarto Kids.

Text © 2020 by Quarto Publishing Group USA Inc.

First published in 2020 by Wellfleet Press,
an imprint of The Quarto Group,
142 West 36th Street, 4th Floor
New York, NY 10018, USA
T (212) 779-4972 F (212) 779-6058
www.QuartoKnows.com

Wellfleet titles are also available at discount for retail, wholesale, promotional, and bulk purchase. For details, contact the Special Sales Manager by email at specialsales@quarto.com or by mail at The Quarto Group, Attn: Special Sales Manager, 100 Cummings Center Suite 265D, Beverly, MA 01915 USA.

10 9 8 7 6 5 4 3

ISBN: 978-1-57715-191-3

Library of Congress Cataloging-in-Publication Data

Names: McElroy, D. R. (Debra R.), author.
Title: Superstitions : a handbook of folklore, myths, and legends from
   around the world / D.R. McElroy.
Description: New York, NY : Wellfleet Press, 2020. | Includes index. |
   Summary: "Superstitions: A Handbook of Folklore, Myths, and Legends from
   around the World is your definitive reference to the history of
   superstitions, traditions, myths, and folklore from around the world"--
   Provided by publisher.
Identifiers: LCCN 2019052158 (print) | LCCN 2019052159 (ebook) | ISBN
   9781577151913 (hardcover) | ISBN 9780760366295 (ebook)
Subjects: LCSH: Superstition. | Folklore. | Mythology. | Legends.
Classification: LCC GR81 .M38 2020 (print) | LCC GR81 (ebook) | DDC
   398.2--dc23
LC record available at https://lccn.loc.gov/2019052158
LC ebook record available at https://lccn.loc.gov/2019052159

Group Publisher: Rage Kindelsperger
Creative Director: Laura Drew
Managing Editor: Cara Donaldson
Senior Editor: John Foster
Art Director: Cindy Samargia Laun
Cover Design: Laura Klynstra
Interior Design: Tandem Books

Printed in China

SUPERSTITIONS

A HANDBOOK OF
FOLKLORE,
MYTHS, AND LEGENDS
FROM AROUND THE WORLD

D.R. McELROY

WELLFLEET
PRESS

CONTENTS

INTRODUCTION

Do you think black cats are "unlucky"? It is a fact that adoptions of black cats are much less frequent than those of non-black cats. Surprised? Medical facilities routinely report that the number of accidents with injury goes way up during periods of a full moon. And you've likely heard the old wives' tale that it is unlucky for the groom to see the bride in her wedding dress before the wedding ceremony.

The question that begs to be answered is why are humans superstitious? There's an argument to be made that superstitions arose from humanity's need to exert control over a confusing and chaotic world. Seems reasonable, but how are black cats something that we can control? Historically, the ancient Egyptians revered all cats as sacred regardless of color. Cats controlled the vermin populations and helped prevent the spread of disease, as well as prevented small creatures from eating up the stores of grain needed to ward off starvation. There is a legend that King Charles I of England had a black pet cat that he adored so much that when it died the king proclaimed all of his luck had perished as well. The story claims that Charles I was arrested the very next day for treason, proving that his cat had lucky (or unlucky!) abilities.

Time is a factor in the development of superstitions as well. Something that may have started out as a cautionary tale, such as the prohibition against opening umbrellas indoors, eventually morphs into a general bit of "common sense" that we still take for granted. In the case of umbrellas, in their early days of development umbrellas were huge, bulky, and awkward, with powerful springs attached to their opening mechanism. A running child could be seriously injured—or a fragile glass ornament shattered—by the sudden deployment of a steel-ribbed bumbershoot indoors where it is least expected. As time passes, the *reason* for the prohibition may be lost, but the prohibition remains.

While the development of superstitions and myths is a fascinating study, this book would be a thousand pages long if we tried to discern the cause or development behind each story here. We will look at the development of certain practices where it is particularly fascinating or relevant.

So, have you ever wondered what the difference is between a myth and a superstition? Are legends and folk tales the same thing? Where did all of these things come from? Let's look at each one.

Superstition: a widely held, but unsubstantiated belief in supernatural causation of outcomes related to particular odd rituals. For example, if you spill the salt but quickly throw a pinch of it over your left shoulder, it is believed that bad luck will be avoided. These practices are commonly attached to beliefs in prophecy, luck, or magic. Certain religious practices may be labeled "superstition" if the religion associated with them is not the predominate religion of the region (for example, voodoo in the largely Christian United States).

Myth: a traditional story used to explain the history of a people or a natural phenomenon such as storms or earthquakes, which typically involves supernatural beings and events. The pantheon of ancient Greek and Roman gods and goddesses is an example of the mythology of a civilization. Myths are frequently associated with religion, but mythology is only a part of what defines religion. Other parts are ritual, doctrine, belief or faith, and institutionalization.

Legend: a popular or traditional story usually associated with a particular person or place, sometimes believed to be part of a true history of a people but without substantiated evidence of such. The tales of King Arthur and his Knights of the Round Table are excellent examples of legend; while an historical figure such as Arthur *may* have existed in ancient Britain, there is little actual proof as to who he might have been.

Folklore: traditional customs, beliefs, and stories of a particular community which are passed down from generation to generation through oral discourse. This is the main difference between folklore (and folk tales) and other traditions—the verbal communication of the stories among community members. The stories of Pecos Bill and Paul Bunyan in the US are examples of folklore.

Here are a couple of other definitions that might be useful:

Fable: a short story, frequently featuring animal characters, that is used to teach a moral lesson. Think "The Fox and the Grapes" or "The Scorpion and the Frog" from *Aesop's Fables*.

Parable: similar to a fable, except that parables use *human* characters instead of animals or inanimate objects to teach the lesson. Jesus used parables like the Prodigal Son to communicate his message of love. Just to be clear, in many regions of the world, Jesus himself is a myth or a legend and not a historical figure.

Urban legend (also urban myth): unique in that they are entertaining stories passed off as "factual"; the internet has caused such stories to gain wide-spread believers, whereas such stories tended to spread by word-of-mouth much more slowly in years past. Examples of urban legends are "Alligators in the Sewers," the "Rattlesnake in the Fur Coat," the "Hook Man" tales (which were formerly spread as campfire stories), and the "Neiman Marcus Cookie Recipe." One of the newest urban legends is "Slender Man," which was made into a recent movie.

These definitions help us identify various types of stories, but they are not critical unless one is a professor of folklore or some such. Just keep in mind that what these stories have in common is that they are *fiction* due to their general lack of historical evidence.

This book is going to examine some of the myths and superstitions from around the world. Some you may be familiar with while some may be completely new to you. Hopefully, you will find this book entertaining and enlightening, whether you believe the stories or not. The stories are grouped by continent, but not every country in each continent will be listed—sadly, there just isn't room for all of them!

This book—for the sake of simplicity and clarity—will contain selections from the enormous body of myth and superstition. The reader may find that the stories they know from their own culture might be expressed differently (including name changes and godly powers) than the ones they grew up with. Hopefully, readers can find joy in the variety while learning about different aspects of familiar tales.

AFRICA

Africa remains a mysterious and unknown world to most Westerners. At once vast and modest, empty and lush, Africa remains an enigma in history and in modern times. Historical Africa was the realm of mighty kings, rich in material wealth and rulers of enormous tracts. Incredible civilizations rose and fell here while much of the rest of the world was still living in caves. African mythology draws from a very deep well of religious and political experience; indeed, no other land holds such lasting imagery and traditions as those of this incredible place.

The African continent is the second-largest land mass in the world, covering nearly 12 million square miles (20 percent of all land on earth). It is also the second most populous continent (behind Asia) containing over 1.2 billion people—who speak about two thousand different native languages. This huge variety makes listing mythologies difficult since even if two groups have the same mythology, the names and other details in the legends may vary widely. Africa is the only continent to span all four hemispheres of the earth. The East African Rift zone, also called the Great Rift Valley, extends from the Jordan River through the Dead Sea, the Red Sea, and Kenya, and all the way to Mozambique. The area is referred to as the "cradle of civilization," due to the huge amount of archaeological and anthropological development that took place there.

There is a striking difference between countries in Africa based on geography. Countries in the northern part of the continent (including Algeria, Morocco, Egypt, Libya, and Tunisia) are usually grouped together with Middle Eastern countries (such as Iran, Iraq, Syria, and Saudi Arabia) to form a complex referred to as North Africa and the Middle East. Countries outside of this complex—those mainly south of the Sahara Desert, including South Africa, Nigeria, Kenya, and the Republic of the Congo, as well as numerous island nations near the African coast—are considered Sub-Saharan Africa. Israel, while it resides in the Middle East, is much more politically and economically aligned with the US and Europe; therefore, it is usually left out of conversations about the area.

African Mythical Monsters

Here are some of the creepiest, scariest monsters from various African mythologies.

⊰ Adze ⊱
Ghana

Adze is a shape-shifting insect; this creature attacks children while in its firefly form and drains their young, vital blood. If caught in the act, the firefly changes into a human form with the power to possess the souls of other humans. The possessed enter a zombie-like state, completely under the control of the Adze. Eventually, the possessed person will die.

⊰ Agogwe ⊱
East Africa

An Agogwe is a small biped with red or yellowish skin topped with orangey hair that lives in the remote forests of the region. While not technically monsters, the Agogwe are quite mysterious, and have allegedly been spotted, according to East African folklore. One of the first recorded sightings by a non-African occurred in the nineteenth century, when a British army officer on a hunting expedition came across two of the creatures. His guide said they were called Agogwe; the hunter subsequently tried to track the creatures without success. Various sightings continued, with a number coming from the area of Mozambique. While several theories about the creatures have been put forth (including that they are part of a "lost tribe" of pygmies), it seems more likely that they would be a type of orangutan (based on their size and coloring) which may have since become extinct.

⊰ BILOKO ⊱
ZAIRE

The Biloko are devious, dwarvish spirits of the rainforest—resentful ancestor
entities that envy the living. They dwell in hollow trees and zealously guard the
creatures of the forest from hunters foolish enough to enter. Biloko are bald
creatures with razor-like claws and gnashing teeth in a jaw that can open wide
enough to swallow an entire human being whole. They also have the power to
hypnotize their prey before devouring them.

⊰ GROOTSLANG ⊱
SOUTH AFRICA

From the Richtersveld cave in South Africa comes the story of the giant serpent,
Grootslang. The name Grootslang comes from Afrikaans (the primary language of
South Africa) and means "great snake." Stories of this monster go back centuries,
describing a creature with the body of a snake and the head of an elephant. The
skin is greyish green and scaly, and the eyes are a combination of elephant and
snake eyes. It also possesses elephant ears and a strange, cobra-like hood. They
exhibit venomous elephant tusks and cobra fangs. Like Mamlambo, the Grootslang
have been depicted in ancient cave paintings in the region. Legend states that the
Grootslang was the result of a "mistake" by the gods; when they realized that the
monster they had created was too ferocious to live in the world, they split the
creature into two distinct species of elephants and snakes. However, the original
creature could not be killed and it escaped, becoming the source for all Grootslang
birthed later.

The creatures live in herds, with the mothers and babies staying together for
years while solo males drift away to establish their own herds. Grootslang live in a
cave with no bottom—literally, no one knows where the cave system ends and the
caves have not been fully mapped. Legend states that the cave is full of diamonds,
which the animals zealously guard. If you are cornered by a Grootslang, you might
be able to bargain for your life if you are carrying a sufficient stash of gems that
the creature finds acceptable to trade for your life. Grootslang are omnivorous (like
humans) and seem to bear no ill will beyond their thirst for diamonds.

⊰ INKANYAMBA ⊱
SOUTH AFRICA

Inkanyamba are huge water serpents that have a dorsal fin running the length of their spines, and the head of a horse. They may also possess horns and/or wings. They are usually about 25 feet (7.6 meters) long, but they can grow much larger. Their food of choice is goats and cattle, but they will eat humans if provoked or hungry enough. Inkanyamba are capable of flight and will migrate seasonally to find mates. When flying, they are able to affect the weather, and can cause large thunderstorms, tornados, and hail. The creatures are apparently not terribly bright; they are given to hiding behind waterfalls, and can be fooled into mistaking the blue roof of someone's house for a body of water, subsequently diving right into it. Some Ghanaians will paint their roofs a dark color to prevent this.

⊰ MAMLAMBO ⊱
SOUTH AFRICA

A terrifying monster, Mamlambo is believed to live in the Mzintlava River, and it kills its victims by dragging them into the water and devouring their faces in order to access their brains. Dubbed the "brain sucker," the monster is 60 feet (18 meters) long with a crocodile torso, a long serpentine neck, and a horse-like head. It is said to behave like a snake and to glow with an eerie green bioluminescence at night. It has hypnotic green eyes that can mesmerize anyone who dares make eye contact with it. The creature has been depicted in cave paintings in the region that date back thousands of years. A very similar creature known as Ninki Nanka hails from Gambia. The Mamlambo was blamed as recently as 1990 for several deaths in the Mzintlava River, though authorities were not convinced the creature was responsible.

⊰ NAGA ⊱
NORTH AFRICA

Naga is a generic term used by the peoples of North Africa, Asia, and Polynesia to describe gigantic sea serpents that typically resemble snakes—specifically cobras. Naga is a Sanskrit word meaning "snake" or "cobra." Naga (both singular and plural) frequently are part animal and part human; usually it has a human head and torso on the body of a snake. These creatures are deeply magical and fiendishly aggressive, doing their best to terrify and consume sailors of the seas. Naga are particularly prominent in Hindu and Buddhist mythology.

⊰ NYAMI NYAMI ⊱
ZAMBIA

The Nyami Nyami is a dragon-like god of the mighty Zambezi River, the fourth-largest river system in Africa. Though the god is ancient, the most recent tale of his power dates from the mid-twentieth century and the building of the Kariba Dam. The Batonga people, who were displaced by the building of the dam in 1956, believed that Nyami Nyami would prevent it from being built, thus allowing them to return to their ancestral homeland. Just a year into its construction, a catastrophic flood occurred, killing several workers and destroying the partially built dam. Loved ones of the dead waited days for the bodies to be recovered, until Batongan elders told them that Nyami Nyami would only release the bodies after a sacrifice had been made to him. A calf was slaughtered in his name and left on the river bank; the next day, the bodies of the workers were found in the same spot, and the calf's body was gone.

African Gods and Goddesses

Some of the powerful African deities around the continent include the following.

⚞ Anansi ⚟
Ghana

Anansi is the best known of all the African gods; he is usually depicted as a spider and is the primary trickster god of West Africa and the Caribbean. There are hundreds of stories of Anansi's deeds (and misdeeds) as he tries to trick humanity into following his wicked ways. For this reason, Anansi is credited with the gifts of persuasion, guile, charm, and cleverness. He also personifies greed and materialism.

Some sources say that Anansi stories are so well preserved because they were cherished as a means of subversive behavior and resistance among enslaved Ashanti and other African peoples in the New World. Though Anansi often failed in the tales, he continued to connive and strive to meet his ends, giving the enslaved hope in their continued struggle to be free.

A typical Anansi tale is how the trickster brought stories to the world by bargaining with the creator god Nyame, and performing seemingly impossible tasks via his gifts of charm and cleverness of speech. Thus, Anansi became the god of stories. In another fable, Anansi accidentally spreads wisdom throughout the world when he drops the pot in which he collected all the wisdom into a river, where it flows to the sea and spreads around the world. It is because of this that everyone has a little bit of wisdom.

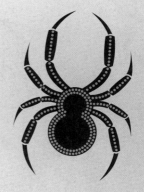

⚹ HUVEANE ⚹
SOUTH AFRICA

Some stories have Huveane as the First Man, while others portray him as a devious trickster god. As the creator of the world, it is said that Huveane was admiring his handiwork in peace and quiet—until humans discovered "the birds and the bees," so to speak. The racket resulting from this discovery actually drove Huveane from the earth; he ascended into the heavens by magically nailing steps into the air itself. Huveane protected his retreat by dislodging each step behind him as he climbed up to the stars, so that no human could climb up after him.

⚹ KAANG ⚹
SOUTHERN AFRICAN CONTINENT

The Bushmen (also Khoi or San) are historic nomads of the southern continent, though most of their number have become farmers in modern times. In legend, Kaang is the creator/destroyer of the earth and all living things. It is said that Kaang's wife gave birth to the first eland (an African antelope), which was carefully nurtured by the god—until his sons somehow accidentally killed the animal. Kaang ordered that the eland's blood be boiled, and the resultant residue scattered across the plains. From these droplets sprang more eland, as well as other creatures of the earth that the Khoi believe were meant for them to hunt and eat to survive.

AFRICAN
LIVING LEGENDS

⊰ MODJADJI ⊱
SOUTH AFRICA/ZIMBABWE

The Modjadji (the spelling varies) dynasty has a long and complicated history, but it officially began with the crowning of the first Modjadji Rain Queen, Maselekwane Modjadji I, in 1800. The Rain Queens are all descended from this royal line, and the title is hereditary, passed from mother to designated daughter. The Rain Queen has the magical power of creating rain, and she has historically been consulted by tribal leaders that include the Zulu King Shaka and former South African President Nelson Mandela. The youngest Rain Queen ever crowned was Makobo Caroline Modjadji VI in 2003 at the young age of twenty-five. She died mysteriously two years later, leaving a five-month-old daughter to (someday) inherit the title. Queen Makobo was considered a rebellious and "troublesome" person who flaunted tradition and refused to bow down to the council of elders.

NIGERIA

Nigeria is the most densely populated country in Africa, with Ethiopia being the second. Nigeria fits all of her residents (roughly two-thirds of the population of the entire US) into a space about 30 percent larger than the state of Texas. This densely packed population means there is a lot of personal contact amongst people, a situation that could cause stressful living conditions. Dense populations usually exercise great care to ensure personal boundaries are respected and that social conventions are followed. One way to do this is to develop a large number of ritualized practices, including superstitions. What are superstitions, after all, but ritualized practices tied to cautionary tales? These tales give (logical) reasons for people to conform to the rituals. Nigerians are said to be some of the most superstitious people in Africa. Here are some of their beliefs.

IF YOU STUMBLE or otherwise trip over a stone or stump with your left leg, you must turn back from your journey and head home. Not doing so invites the worst luck, including potential loss of the limb or even death on the journey.

IF SOMEONE STEPS over you, that person must step back across in the same manner or you will stop growing, or perhaps lose the body part the person stepped over.

IF YOU HIT a man with a broom, he will become impotent—unless he takes the broom from you and hits you seven times with it in return.

DON'T WHISTLE OR draw water from a well at night. Night whistling is believed to attract snakes to you, while fetching water from the well in darkness will result in an evil spirit slapping you. These particular superstitions may have originated as "safety precautions," as mentioned in the introduction. The dangers lurking in the dark outside the house were very real—and still are in some parts of Africa. Similarly, eating in the dark may invite evil spirits to eat with you, ultimately leading to your death.

DON'T KILL A gecko. The common wall gecko is believed to devour evil spirits that try to enter the house (and also eat many types of undesirable insects). These creatures are harmless to humans, but killing them may cause your house to collapse! By the way, geckos don't have eyelids, so they lick their eyeballs to keep them moist and dirt free.

HEARING AN OWL hoot means that someone in the household will die soon. This particular superstition is very common among many world cultures, not just Africans. It is possible that the belief spread via the worldwide slave trade in the seventeenth to nineteenth centuries.

BLACK CATS ARE evil. Again, the prohibition against these felines is spread across the globe; they are usually believed to be associated with witches and evil spirits or demons.

DON'T DRINK WATER from a coconut or you will immediately become an *olodo* (a moron).

ITCHY PALMS SIGNIFY that good luck is coming to you. This belief may have given rise to the belief that you would soon be receiving money. Therefore, scratching your palms came to signify "pay me," and the term "scratch" became a slang term for money.

IF YOU SPIT on the floor and someone steps on it, you will get a sore throat

IF YOU BEND over and look through your legs while standing, you might see witches.

PREGNANT WOMEN CANNOT walk about in daylight because the evil spirit of daytime might enter their fetus. We've already heard that walking in darkness is unlucky—pregnant women apparently have to stay indoors all the time.

A KING MAY not view a corpse, even that of a relative. Spirits of the dead may take over the body of a king and use his position to wreak havoc on his subjects.

IF YOU PUT your eyelashes in your parents' shoes, they will forget whatever offense you have committed.

IF THE SUN shines while it's raining, it means that a lion is giving birth. If it rains when the sun is shining, it means that a monkey is getting married.

CUT OFF A lizard's head and bury it. Three days later, dig it up and you will find a cache of money. Now, we've already been told NOT to kill geckos, so apparently you must be sure of the species before you go about beheading lizards.

IF SOMEONE BITES you, rub chicken dung on the bite mark and the biter's teeth will rot.

DON'T EAT FOOD that fell on the floor; Satan has already eaten it.

PREGNANT WOMEN SHOULDN'T visit a zoo lest their children wind up looking like monkeys (or some other animal).

IF A BIRD poops on your head, money is coming your way.

THE MIDDLE EAST

In modern times, the name may conjure notions of oil fields, fabulous wealth, and political unrest. Move back in time a hundred years and the focus is on astounding (if controversial) discoveries of hidden tombs, lost cities, and civilizations whose achievements staggered the world.

Egypt likely springs to mind first among these. Ancient when the great dynasties of Asia were still young, Egypt controlled vast territories across the African continent. They were planners, builders, and artisans. They left behind huge mysterious constructions, statues, and idols of gods and kings unknown. Most of what we know about those ancient folk has only been deciphered in the last century, millennia after that civilization went extinct.

The countries of modern-day Iran, Iraq, Israel, and others have their own histories and stories to tell, and we'll look at them, too.

Without going into a discussion about the politics involved in the use of the designation "the Middle East," the term is thought by much of the world to refer to a collection of countries that share a common geographical location—and sometimes a common mythology and heritage. The countries of the Middle East include: Egypt, Lebanon, Palestine, Syria, and Jordan (countries that were formerly referred to as "the Levant"), plus Iraq, Iran, Afghanistan, and the Arabian Peninsula. As previously mentioned, the complete lack of commonality between the peoples of the Middle East and the nation of Israel—with its strong political and economic ties to the West—results in Israel typically being left off the list of countries considered to make up the Middle East. Though much farther to the east geographically, Pakistan's politics qualify that country for inclusion in the Middle East concept.

The first known recorded mythological story (and considered to be the oldest existing piece of literature remaining) is the *Epic of Gilgamesh*, written by ancient Sumerians about 2100 BCE, and surviving in the form of cuneiform tablets. The story is in the form of an epic poem, and it tells of the heroics and failings of the great Sumerian king Gilgamesh (*Bilgamesh* in Sumerian), who was said to have been two-thirds god and one-third human.

Gilgamesh was king of the city-state of Uruk, in Sumer. The abbreviated version of his story has Gilgamesh undertaking a long journey after defying the gods and suffering the death of his best friend. The epic inspired the works of the Greek poet Homer, who used it as the model for his *Odyssey* and Gilgamesh as the inspiration for the character of Odysseus. One of the most interesting parts of the original *Epic* is its details concerning the Great Flood. Nearly all ancient (and many modern) cultures have a flood story, which typically features humanity somehow angering the gods, or god, and suffering the punishment of being wiped from the earth by flood waters. Some scientists theorize that this common mythology arises from the worldwide experience of glacial melting at the end of the last Ice Age. This idea led to the controversial theory of "race memory," in which the traumatic experience of the floods was passed down *genetically* from one generation to the next for millennia.

Another important contribution to ancient Middle Eastern literature was made by a woman—specifically a woman named Enheduanna, who is considered to be the oldest-known author to be referred to by name. While the *Epic of Gilgamesh* was written by persons unknown, Enheduanna is credited with a number of works of epic poetry. She lived in about 2200 BCE in the kingdom of Sumer, where she was a high priestess. She was the daughter of the Akkadian King Sargon the Great (himself the son of a priestess) and Queen Tashlultum. Under Sargon, Akkad would conquer and absorb a great number of Sumerian city-states, including Gilgamesh's Uruk (known by Sargon's time as Ur).

Enheduanna was so important a figure in the literary world of the time that she was tasked with reconciling the pantheon of Sumerian gods with that of the Akkadians, in order to encourage the conquered Sumerian cities to accept Akkadian rule. She succeeded spectacularly at this task and was given responsibility for managing the Temple of Sumeria. She established conventions for writing poetry that would survive to profoundly influence the writing of the Hebrew Bible, as well as many poems and hymns of ancient Greece. She was eventually buried in the Ziggurat of Ur.

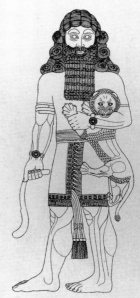

EGYPT

Perhaps no civilization exemplifies the wide range of unusual and curious mythology more than Egypt. While modern Egypt is mostly Muslim, the huge pantheon of gods and goddesses in the ancient civilization of Egypt—nearly all of which combine animal and human features (a convention known as *therianthrophic* depiction)—demonstrates a rich and versatile range of deities for all occasions.

EGYPTIAN GODS AND GODDESSES

The following is a list of the most popular Egyptian gods and goddesses.

⚜ ANAT ⚜

Anat was the goddess of war and consort of Set. She was "imported" from Canaanite mythology, where she had been known as Anath. She seems to have fared better as an Egyptian goddess than as a Canaanite one. See her listing as *Anath* in the Middle Eastern Gods and Goddesses section.

⚜ ANUBIS ⚜

Undoubtedly the Egyptian god most familiar to Western civilization, Anubis was the jackal-headed god of the dead. His role was to guide the deceased to the underworld, where their souls (which resided in their hearts) would be weighed by Osiris, king of the underworld.

⚜ Bast/Bastet ⚜

Bast is a protective goddess, usually depicted as a cat with earrings, or as a woman with the head of a cat. When the Greek civilization came in contact with the Egyptians, the Greeks adapted some of the Egyptian deities to their own pantheon; Bast became known as Ailuros to the Greeks, which is the source of the word *ailurophile,* meaning "cat lover."

⚜ Bes ⚜

This god is usually depicted as a dwarf sticking out his tongue (and facing *front* instead of to the side, as most Egyptian deities are shown). Bes was said to confer protection in childbirth and improve fertility. He also guarded against snakes (which seems curious since the cobra is one of the symbols of royalty in ancient Egypt).

⚜ Hathor ⚜

A highly prominent goddess, Hathor is the protector of women in childbirth and incarnation of the Milky Way on earth. Hathor is frequently depicted as a hippopotamus, or sometimes a cow. She was the wife of the sun god Ra, and mother of the pharaonic god Horus.

⚜ Horus/Heru/Hor ⚜

Perhaps the most highly revered god in ancient Egypt, Horus was the protector of pharaohs and a role model for young males, as well as King of the Black (rich soil) region of Egypt. Horus is always depicted as a man with the head of a falcon—a bird sacred to pharaohs. Horus had a number of different aspects, including Horus the Avenger, Horus Lord of the Two Lands, and Horus Behudety.

⚓ Isis ⚓

The greatest goddess in the Egyptian pantheon, Isis was the sister/wife of Osiris and daughter of Geb and Nut. Isis had influence over many aspects of Egyptian life, including beer, wind, abundance, the heavens, and magic. She is credited with bringing Osiris back from the dead, and subsequently giving birth to Horus, the protector of pharaohs. Isis is typically depicted as a beautiful woman wearing a sun disk headdress.

⚓ Neith/Nit/Net/Neit ⚓

One of the oldest Egyptian goddesses, Neith predates the period of the great dynasties of Egypt (before 5000 BCE). Usually depicted as a weaver of cloth (especially the bandages used to wrap mummies), Neith became associated with the goddess Athena of the Greeks. She is sometimes shown wearing the Red Crown of Lower Egypt. Neith is one of the few gods not associated with an animal.

⊰ Osiris ⊱

Osiris was the king of the underworld, father of Horus. He is usually depicted as a pharaoh wearing a crown and the horns of a ram, carrying a crook and flail (the scepters of pharaohs), and having the lower half of his body wrapped in the bandages of a mummy. Often, his skin is green.

⊰ Ra/Re ⊱

Ra was the sun god and the god of everything. He was a mentor to Horus, and he is typically depicted as a man with a sun disk on his head, or sometimes as a man with the head of a falcon (which may cause him to be confused with Horus).

⊰ Set/Seti/Seth ⊱

Set was the god of chaos and brother/murderer of Osiris. Set was king of the red (desert) region of Egypt and the agent of fierce storms. He is usually depicted as various composite animals—especially as a man with the head of an unknown creature (perhaps now extinct) that is called the "Set animal" or the "Typhonic beast." It resembles an aardvark with floppy donkey ears.

Egyptian Mythical Monsters

In addition to gods, Egypt had a number of outright monsters to deal with, many of them intent upon eating the unwary and unprotected.

⊰ Ammit ⊱
Devourer of the Dead

This creature (like many in Egyptian mythology) was a chimera—a mixture of parts from different animals. Ammit was said to have a crocodile head, front body of a lion, and forebody of a hippo. Ammit's job was to eat the heart of those judged unworthy by Osiris, thus casting the soul of the unfortunate into the fires of limbo.

⊰ Apep ⊱
Enemy of Light

Depicted as a gigantic serpent, Apep was said to battle Ra every morning for control of the coming day. The rising sun was the signal that Ra had defeated the serpent yet again.

⊰ Bennu ⊱
the Bird God

Considered by some scholars to be the source of the legend of the Phoenix, Bennu was a familiar of Ra and the spirit that gave life to all of creation. Often depicted as a wading bird such as a crane, Bennu was also associated with rebirth and renewal.

⊨ GRIFFIN ⊨

Although its exact origins are lost, the Griffin is mentioned in both ancient Persian and Egyptian texts. The Griffin is a chimera with the head, wings, and front talons of an eagle, and the body of a lion. This creature symbolizes kingship, war, and guardianship (particularly over troves of treasure).

⊨ MA'AT ⊨

Not strictly a monster nor a goddess, Ma'at was the daughter of the sun god Ra, and she represented all that was right, good, harmonious, truthful, and just. Ma'at was not just a goddess but also a concept similar to "The Force" in the *Star Wars*™ movies. Ma'at was the harmony and natural order of the universe that bound everything together; it was the infinite cycles of flooding of the Nile, the continuation of pharaonic power, and the cosmic opposite of *Isfet* (chaos). It was the duty of the pharaoh to maintain Ma'at for his people and his kingdom.

Ma'at was usually depicted as an ostrich feather, or a woman with a feather in her hair. It was one of her feathers that was weighed against the heart of the recently deceased in the underworld. If the heart weighed more than the feather, it was deemed unworthy and fed to Ammit, while the soul of the unfortunate deceased was cast into the fiery pit.

⊰ Serpopard ⊱

This chimera was composed of the head
and neck of a serpent and the body of
a leopard. The meaning attached to
this creature has been lost to history,
but its image appears on Egyptian and
Mesopotamian art dating back to 5000
BCE. Some scholars believe it to be a
symbol of chaos and uncertainty, while
others believe it might be related to male
bonding and virility.

⊰ Uraeus ⊱
the Great Cobra
of the Pharaohs

The image of the rearing cobra Uraeus has its origins in the depths of ancient
Egyptian history. The cobra was associated with the very old goddess Wadjet, who
ruled Lower Egypt and represented the fertility of the Nile Delta. At about the
same time in history, the fertility goddess of Upper Egypt was known as Nehkbet,
and her symbol was the white vulture. Around 3000 BCE, the Upper and Lower
kingdoms were unified into one country, and, in a gesture of reconciliation, the
cobra and the vulture were both depicted on the new "double crown" of the
pharaoh. The Egyptian name for the double crown was the *pschent*.

Middle Eastern Gods and Goddesses

A note about Middle Eastern gods and goddesses: the Middle East historically was (and still maintains) a melding of various cultural practices. It is not uncommon to find that a particular deity was popular in many different countries at varying times in history. The names are frequently changed or have variations in spelling, and sometimes the attributes of the deities will fluctuate. In the interest of trying for simplification, most of the gods and goddesses here will have a single listing, with their various names and attributes mentioned. Also of note, the deities listed here are (mostly) from pre-Islamic and pre-Christian influences. The roots of the Jewish religion can be found among these gods.

AHRIMAN/AKUMAN/AKO-MAINYU/ANGRA MAINYU/ANRA MAINIIU
ZOROASTRIAN

Ahriman was the bringer of all evil, nemesis of Ahura Mazda, the devil. A dark and stinking supreme demon, he was the inspiration for the Jewish Satan. He will be opposed in the final battle at the end of time by Ahura Mazda.

AHURA MAZDA/AHURAMAZDA/ORMAZD/ ORMIZD/MAZDA/OROMASDES
ZOROASTRIAN

Ahura Mazda was the supreme creator of the universe, god of light and truth, source of all good. The god would become known as Mithras to the Roman legions, who zealously supported his cult in Roman Britain. Zoroastrianism is an ancient religion predating Judaism and Christianity, which flourished in and around ancient Persia (modern-day Iran). It was founded by Zoroaster (also Zarathustra) and survives to this day, despite the loss of nearly all of its sacred scriptures in the fire at the Library of Alexandria. Its concept of a single god and the eternal battle between the agents of good and evil profoundly influenced the later developments of Judaism and Christianity. Ahura Mazda was attended by the Amesha Spenta—holy spirits of goodness, which were half god and half angel and were the intermediaries between Ahura Mazda and humanity. There were seven of them, and they each had an allotted function:

- AMERETAT -
IMMORTALITY

- KHSHATHRA-VAIRYA -
PERFECT SOCIETY

- SPENTA-ARMAIT -
DEVOTION

- SRAOSHA -
OBEDIENCE

- ASHA-VAHISHTA -
TRUTH

- VOHU-MANAH -
RIGHTEOUS THINKING

- HAURVATAT -
WHOLENESS

⊰ ANAHIT ⊱
ARMENIA

Goddess of fertility, wisdom, healing, and water, Anahit began as a war goddess similar to Anahita (Persia), and was considered to be the benefactor of humanity.

⊰ ANATH/ASTARTE/ASHTORETH ⊱
CANAAN/PHOENICIA

Goddess of fertility and sexuality, as well as war, and sister/wife of Baal, Anath was frequently depicted as a cow (linking to the ancient practice listed in the Christian Bible of bull worship, and perhaps developing into the Hindu belief that cows are sacred). She embarrassed herself by failing in her pursuit of a special bow, which turned out to be holding up the sky. When the heavens collapsed onto the earth, she was forced to ask El (the Creator god, who may or may not have been the progenitor of the Hebrew god Yahweh) for help. Perhaps her humiliation was too much, as she seems to have migrated to Egypt and become the goddess Anat. Babylonians knew her as Ishtar, although Ishtar is also believed to be associated with the moon goddess Sin/Nanna.

⊲ ARAMAZD ⊳
ARMENIA

Aramazd was the supreme god and Creator, patron of rain, fertility, and abundance. He was also father of gods, including Anahit (goddess of fertility and war), Mihr (god of the sun and the light of Heaven), and Nane (mother goddess, and goddess of war and wisdom). Aramazd was sometimes listed as the husband of Anahit as well. Aramazd was the Armenian version of the Old Persian god Ahura Mazda.

⊲ ARINNA/ARINIDDU ⊳
HITTITE

Arinna was the goddess of the sun. Arinna offered protection from war and disaster, ensuring happiness and the good life while the sun shone. Her consort was a mysterious (yet fearsomely powerful) storm god whose name has been lost to history. Some scholars believe that this storm god was ultimately absorbed into the god Teshub.

⊲ ASHUR ⊳
ASSYRIA

Ashur was the god of war, with the body of a lion and the head and (four) wings of an eagle. He was sometimes credited with swooping down from the heavens and "absorbing" Marduk from Babylonia, taking over that god's purview.

⚜ Baal/Ba'al/Baal-Hadad ⚜
Canaan/Phoenicia

Baal was the storm god of war, also known as the "Cloud Monster." Baal had humble beginnings as the stumbling storm god Hadad/Rimmon—also "the Crasher"—who created thunder by bumbling about the heavens. The Babylonians knew him as Adad. Baal overcame his embarrassing beginnings to become the mighty god of war (and also Heroic Deeds, which demonstrates the Canaanites' fever for battle). His consort was Anath.

⚜ Beelzebub/Baal-Zebub/Baal-Zebul/ Beelzebul/Ba'al Zevûv ⚜
Philistine

This being was actually a demon, created by early Jewish leaders, who denigrated the widely-popular god Baal by smearing his name and calling him "Lord of the Flies." This tactic was highly successful, as the Philistines truly despised flies and considered them to be disease-carrying agents of Satan.

⚜ Ereshkigal/Allatu ⚜
Babylonia

Ereshkigal was the goddess of the underworld, death, darkness, and dust. She was the sister of Ishtar and was prone to angry outbursts, depression, and moodiness (understandable when you are the sister of the beautiful, magical Ishtar!). It is said that her lips turned black when she was about to have a fit. Her consort was Nergal.

⚜ Ishtar/Istar ⚜
Akkad/Babylonia

Ishtar was the all-powerful goddess of love, sex, fertility, and war. When the Akkadians conquered Sumer, they appropriated most of the Sumerian pantheon as well, which helped mollify the surviving Sumerians and bend them to Akkadian

rule. Ishtar took over the Sumerian goddess Nanna's role as keeper of the moon. Ishtar is often represented by an eight-pointed star called the Evening Star (counterpoint of the sun). Ishtar's influence was so vast that she was known in many cultures by many names. In addition to Nanna/Inanna in Sumer, she was Astarte or Ashtoreth in Canaan/Phoenicia, Isis in Egypt, Aphrodite in Greece, and Venus in the Empire of Rome. The consort of Ishtar was Tammuz, god of agriculture and rebirth.

⊰ MARDUK ⊱
BABYLONIA

As the supreme god, fertility god, and all-mighty holy leader, Marduk was a much-loved god at the top of the Babylonian pantheon and the ultimate possessor of the Tablet of Destinies. Unfortunately for the Babylonians, he was somehow "stolen" by the Assyrians, causing massive crop failures and wars—which the Babylonians typically lost. He was usually depicted as having a beard and wearing a curious hat that looked like either a turkey leg or a birthday cake.

⊰ Nergal ⊱
Babylonia

God of the underworld, Nergal was a literal bull who got his underworld crown by wresting the throne from Ereshkigal, then offering to share it with her.

⊰ Saoshyant/Saohyant/Saošiiant ⊱
Zoroastrian

Saoshyant was the messiah and god of renewal, who would appear at the end of time to take the faithful followers of Ahura Mazda off to a big party, while the followers of Ahriman and the nonbelievers perished in hell-fire. He was the precursor of Jesus Christ.

⊰ Sin/Nanna/Inanna ⊱
Sumer/Akkad

Enheduanna was the priestess for this moon goddess. In the Semitic language of the Akkadians, the moon goddess was named Sin (Sumerian Nanna or Inanna). Sin/Nanna is the deity to whom the famous Ziggurat of Ur was dedicated. Sin/Nanna would eventually become known as Ishtar to the Babylonians, and as Aphrodite to the Greeks.

⊰ Yahweh ⊱
Jewish

Yahweh is the one true god of the Israelites, the god of the Torah, supreme being and Creator. Yahweh selected the Israelites to be his "chosen people," the Israelites did not choose him. This made Yahweh unique among gods. He was a vengeful and jealous god, who demanded obeisance and lots of sacrifices. After Moses led the children of Israel to freedom—where they argued and complained and fell into idolatry—Yahweh spent hundreds of years testing and tormenting his chosen ones, until the birth of Jesus changed everything. Old Testament god Yahweh became New Testament Jehovah, and his followers spread Christianity across the globe.

Middle Eastern Mythical Monsters

In the following section, some of the more well-known Middle Eastern mythical monsters are presented.

⚜ Al Anqa'a ⚜
Arabia

Mentioned in ancient Arabian legends, this creature's name means "the long-necked one." Al Anqa'a is a giant bird-like animal capable of carrying away almost anything, including humans, presumably to eat them. It is not strictly a "monster," but a giant, man-eating bird sounds pretty terrifying!

⚜ Al Bahmout ⚜
Arabia

Although not strictly a monster, this beast is variously described as an enormous whale/bull/elephant that carries the mythical Seven Earths upon its back.

⚜ Al Rukh/Roc ⚜
Arabia

Another product of *One Thousand and One Nights*, this bird was even more enormous than Al Anqa'a, and was capable of carrying off even elephants and rhinos! Al Rukh gave his name to the European rook, a very large, crow-like bird with a whitish face and bill that stands out prominently against its black body. To the ancient Persians it was known as Sharukh (various spellings).

⚔ Anzu/Anzû/Imdugud/Zu ⚔
Assyria

Anzu is a golden eagle with the head of a lion, and he is the bringer of storms and wind. Anzu was involved in the continued attempts at the theft of the so-called Tablet of Destiny (or Tablet of the Destinies), which would make whoever possessed them all-knowing and all-powerful—a true god. Why such a powerful object existed in the first place is inexplicable.

⚔ Djinn ⚔
Persia, India, Arabia

Made famous by the stories of *One Thousand and One Nights*, the Djinn are magical creatures that can assume the form of any creature—animal or human. Djinn can be large or small, but they have a reputation for being hostile. Many stories tell of captive "genies" who trick their masters when granting three magical wishes.

⚔ Efrit ⚔
Arabia

Efrit are creatures that are essentially demonic, but can change to good. They live in complex societies, and are intelligent and cunning.

⚔ Falak ⚔
Arabia

Falak is a massive subterranean serpent who will emerge from the underworld at the end of time to torture sinners.

⚔ Ghol/al gohl/ghoul ⚔
Arabia

Ghol are zombie-esque demons who haunt cemeteries and prey on humans; the creatures are nocturnal. The name derives from the Arabic *ras al-gul*, "head of the ogre" (exact English translation: "demon star").

⚔ GOLEM ⚕
KABBALAH JUDAISM

This somewhat familiar creature is a "poppet,"—a creature made from inert materials (frequently clay or earth) in the vague shape of a human, which is brought to a zombie-like life by a wizard or other powerful mage through the use of spells and rituals. The creature has no conscience and no mind of its own; it does its master's bidding—until the master is no longer able to control it, whereupon it usually destroys its master. The golem may be large or small, though since it is frequently sent to do evil, a large size is more useful.

⚔ HEDAMMU/APŠE ⚕
TURKEY/ANATOLIA

Hedammu was a sea-dragon of Hurrian-Hittite mythology that possessed a huge appetite and nearly devoured the goddess Ishtar, before succumbing to her ample charms. He was known as Illuyanka to the Hittites, and Typhon to the Greeks.

⚔ ILLUYANKA ⚕
HITTITE

Illuyanka is a sea serpent-like dragon slain by the god of the sky and storms, Tarhunna. Tarhunna was Terhunz to the Anatolians, and Teshub to the Hurrians (as well as Zeus to the Greeks, who famously battled the serpent-monster Typhon).

⚔ LEVIATHAN ⚕
HEBREW

In the Hebrew Bible, the Leviathan is a giant sea monster (described as a whale) that tests the faithful Job. Ultimately, it is defeated by Yahweh. The monster correlates to the Canaanite Lotan, the Greek Typhon, the Indian Vritra, and the Norse Jörmungandr. These are all "world serpents" an archetype that represents chaos and the duality of good and evil.

⚓ Lilith ⚓
Babylonian/Jewish

Lilith is a powerful demon seductress whose name derives from the Babylonian word meaning "night monster" or "night hag." Lilith is declared to be Adam's first wife in Jewish folklore, made from the same clay as he was, rather than from his rib, as Eve would be. Lilith refused to be subservient to Adam and left him in the Garden of Eden; afterwards, she coupled with the archangel Samael. Samael (whose name in Hebrew means "Poison of God" or "Venom of God") would become Ha-Satan, the Archangel of Death in the Talmud. Some stories have Lilith later becoming a demon succubus.

⚓ Manticore ⚓
Persia

Manticore is a man-eating creature with the head of a human, the body of a lion, and the tail of a scorpion. The beast stings its prey with its deadly tail, and then consumes it whole with the help of three rows of sharp teeth. Similar to the Egyptian sphinx (not the riddle-asking one), depictions of the beast were popular in medieval Europe, thanks to the Crusades.

⚓ Nesnas ⚓
Yemen

Nesnas is a hideous creature in the form of a man who is missing half of his body, and has the tail of a lamb.

⚓ Qareen ⚓
Arabia

A sort of doppelgänger of Djinn, Qareen are creatures that exist in a parallel realm of the Djinn. They may come and sit upon your shoulder, tempting you to sin. They are known as Fravashi in the Zoroastrian religion.

⚓ Qarînah ⚓
Arabia

The equivalent of a succubus/incubus, this demon was said to be invisible to all but those who possessed the "second sight;" these mystics saw the creature in the form of a dog or cat.

⚔ SHAHBAZ ⚔
PERSIA/IRAN

Meaning "royal falcon" in Old Persian, Shahbaz was a huge eagle-god that helped the ancient Iranians. An agent of good, it later served as the emblem on the royal standard of Cyrus the Great, founder of the Achaemenid Empire.

⚔ SUCCUBUS ⚔
HEBREW

Succubus was a female demon (male version is incubus) who lured the unwary to the sin of extramarital sex. The demon was typically attractive, the better to seduce its prey. Coitus with succubi/incubi was often addictive, and could even lead to death. The unfortunate parents of a deformed baby were said to have been visited by a succubus/incubus.

⚔ WEREHYENA ⚔
UNKNOWN MIDDLE EASTERN

Like werewolves, Werehyena creatures are humans who transform into hyenas, which can then walk on two legs. They are brutal and ruthless, and they are much larger than regular hyenas.

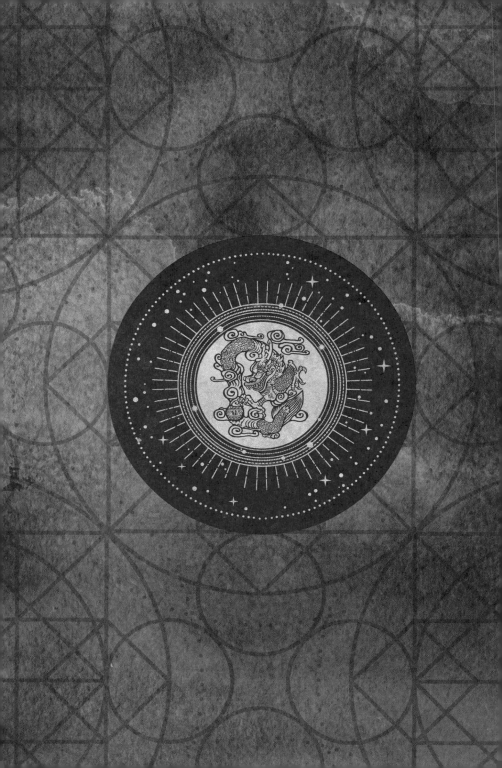

Asia

Asia remained isolated from the West for thousands of years. The cultural traditions and mythologies that arose here were largely unaffected by historical events in the rest of the world. Written records of ancient Asian beliefs begin thousands of years later than those in Africa; the Indian *Rigveda* extends as far back as about 2000 BCE. The Near Eastern Sumerian civilization is credited with inventing the first alphabet, moving the world away from pictographic-type writing. Asian myths derive from various polytheistic religions, and those practices remain largely unaffected by the spread of Christianity even today.

Asian mythology and legends are some of the oldest in recorded history. Countries such as China, Mongolia, Russia, Japan, and Turkey offer stories with themes so elemental that they have permeated the mythologies of Europe and the Americas as well. For example, the *Ramayana* is an Indian epic poem written sometime around 300 BCE which describes the heroics of the god Rama and his love for Sita, a princess who becomes his wife. From China came *The Art of War*, written by Chinese general Sun Tzu/Sunzi between 500 and 400 BCE. This book is still widely read and influential in business boardrooms around the world. Written about the same time period, the *Analects of Confucius* set forth many of the philosophies and social constructs that still govern modern Chinese cultural and beliefs. The vastness and variety of Asian countries prohibits a complete examination of Asian mythology in this section. Our discussion of some of these stories will be mostly limited to the largest or most densely populated countries.

CHINA

China has more people living in it than any country in the world. The earliest of Chinese governments dates to about 2100 BCE and is referred to as the Xia Dynasty. Subsequent dynasties succeeded each other until the Chinese Republic replaced them in the 1911 Xinhai Revolution. In 1949, the People's Republic of China was proclaimed by the Communist Party of China, and is the current government. Chinese mythology is rich, and permeates the mythologies of a number of other Asian countries, including Japan, Korea, and Turkey. Here are some interesting Chinese myths and legends.

CHINESE MYTHICAL MONSTERS

There is a huge pantheon of Chinese creatures of myth. Some of the most interesting follow.

⊰ DENGLONG 蹬龙 ⊱
ALSO WANGTIANHOU 望天吼,
CHAOTIANHOU 朝天吼, OR HOU 犼

This creature is celebrated as one of the most powerful and auspicious symbols in Chinese mythology. The Denglong is a son of the Dragon King, and can defeat other dragons in battle with its fiery breath—and then eat their brains. The Denglong has ten specific characteristics: the horns of a deer, head of a camel, ears of a cat, eyes of a shrimp, mouth of a donkey, mane of a lion, neck of a snake, belly of a *shen* (a clam-like creature), scales of a koi, front claws of an eagle, and rear paws of a tiger. The Denglong can hover like a hummingbird and portends peace and prosperity for the kingdom; thus, it is often associated with emperors.

⚛ LUNG/LONG/LOONG DRAGON ⚛

This is another creature associated with emperors, but only in its five-clawed form. Normally the Lung has four claws, and specific characteristics similar to the Denglong. The dragon has long been a symbol of strength, wisdom, and good character; it is considered a high honor to be compared to a dragon. There are over a hundred different dragons in Chinese mythology. Just a few are listed below.

JIAOLONG (Chinese: 蛟龍 "crocodile dragon"): hornless or scaled, king and defender of all aquatic animals.

TIANLONG (Chinese: 天龍 "heavenly dragon"): celestial dragon that guards heavenly palaces and pulls divine chariots; also a name for the constellation Draco.

YINGLONG (Chinese: 應龍 "responding dragon"): winged dragon associated with rains and floods.

FUZANGLONG (Chinese: 伏藏龍 "hidden treasure dragon"): underworld guardian of precious metals and jewels; associated with volcanoes.

HUANGLONG (Chinese: 黃龍 "yellow dragon"): hornless dragon representing the emperor.

ZHULONG (Chinese: 燭龍 "torch dragon"): a giant red dragon solar deity. It supposedly had a human face on a snake body; it created day and night by opening and closing its eyes, and it created seasonal winds by breathing.

CHILONG (Chinese: 螭龍 "demon dragon"): the Chinese word *chi* means either "hornless dragon" or "mountain demon."

JAPAN

Japan is a country made up of about seven thousand islands, of which Honshu is the largest. Japanese, Chinese, and Korean peoples share a common genealogy, and much of their culture, languages, and traditions are similar as well. Similar enough, in fact, that these countries have developed a unilateral alphabet known as kanji (*hanja* in Korean), which combines those characters shared between the different languages. Utilization of kanji has exploded exponentially in the twenty-first century with the widespread use of the internet.

When we look at Japanese culture and mythology, it isn't a surprise to see numerous similarities to Chinese and Korean traditions. For example, the superstition around the number four being unlucky is for the same reason in both Japan and China: the word for "four" sounds the same as the word for "death," making the number four terribly unlucky. There is also a curious superstition surrounding the use of electric fans. Though found in Japanese culture, too, this particular superstition is prevalent in Korean culture, where it is thought that sleeping in an otherwise unventilated room with an electric fan blowing on you can cause death. This belief seems to have arisen at about the same time as the introduction of the electric room fan to Asia; perhaps it is a result of mistrust of "Western" technology or just a reaction to the novelty of electricity in general. Either way, this superstition persists in Korea and parts of Japan even today.

The Japanese religion of Shinto is animistic—that is, every living and non-living thing has a spirit (referred to as *musubi* 結び). Kami (神) are the pantheon of spirits and phenomena that are worshipped. Many of these spirits are associated with animals, which play an important part in Japanese mythology.

Japanese Gods and Goddesses

Since everything has a spirit in Shintoism, there aren't many supreme gods and goddesses. Here are a few.

⊰ Amaterasu-ōmikami ⊱
天照大神

Amaterasu is the is all-powerful goddess of the sun and the Universe.

⊰ Bishamon ⊱
毘沙門

Bishamon is the protector of human life, fighter of evil, and bringer of good fortune.

⊰ Hachiman no kami ⊱
八幡神

God of war—or, more properly—god of instruction in the arts of war, Hachiman is often symbolized by a dove (ironically, our symbol for peace).

⊰ Inari Ōkami ⊱
稲荷大神

God of sake (pronounced SAH kee), tea, rice, fertility, agriculture, and industry, as well as the patron of swordsmiths and merchants, Inari is typically depicted as androgynous, or either male or female. They are also sometimes referred to as a couplet of three or five individual kami. Inari is the kami of foxes, and the literature on them is extensive; these tales are known as kitsune (キツネ). *Kitsune* means "fox" in Japanese. The familiar red torii gates seen in Japanese gardens were first used to mark the entrance to Inari shrines. Red is the color of foxes. In another interesting twist of mythology, Inari's personal kitsune (which carry the deity's messages and guard their shrines) are depicted as white in color rather than red. White is considered an auspicious color.

The kitsune have their counterparts in Chinese (Huli jing 狸狐精) and Korean (kumiho/gumiho Hangul: 구미호; Hanja: 九尾狐) mythologies as well. There, the fox is often a trickster, causing grief and trouble for dullards, slackers, and drunks, as well as honest, hard scrabble folk. Kitsune are also shape-shifters: the legend of Hakuzōsu 白蔵主 tells of a kitsune who impersonated a Japanese priest.

⊰ KISHIJOTEN ⊱

The goddess of fortune and prosperity, Kishijoten is the sister of Bishamon (also Tamon or Bishamon-ten) and the patron/guardian of geishas. In ancient Japan, Kishijoten was invoked for good luck and success—particularly for children. The historic roots of both Bishamon and Kishijoten can be traced to Hindu deities; Kishijoten corresponds to Lakshmi in Hinduism.

⊰ TAKEHAYA SUSANOO NO MIKOTO ⊱
建速須佐之男命

Also known as Susanoo, god of the sea and storms, Takehaya is the brother of Amaterasu and Tsukuyomi. The legend of these siblings' births is that they were born of the great god Izanagi as he bathed away the pollutants from his visit to the underworld (Yomi-no-kuni 黄泉の国). Amaterasu was born from Izanagi's left eye, Tsukuyomi from his right eye, and Susanoo from the god's nose.

⊰ TSUKUYOMI-NO-MIKOTO ⊱
月読尊

Tsukuyomi is the moon god and brother/husband of Amaterasu. It is interesting to note that the moon deity is *male* and the sun *female* in Japanese mythology, which stands in contrast to the myths of Western civilizations that typically describe the sun as male and the moon as female.

Japanese
Mythological Monsters

Japanese mythology, like Chinese, is rich and varied. Here's a few of the many spirits and monsters.

⊰ Yamata-no-Orochi ⊱

One of the tales of Susanoo involves the sea god traveling up a river until he comes upon an old couple weeping. The couple tell him that their only daughter is to be sacrificed to the hideous sea serpent Yamata-no-Orochi (八岐大蛇 "eight-branched giant snake"). The creature is described as having eight heads and eight tails (eight is a mystical number in Japanese mythology)—its great length being equal to the length of eight valleys and eight hills, its hide covered with moss, its back sporting fir and cypress trees, and its underbelly bloody and inflamed. The couple reveal that they previously had eight daughters, but the monster appeared every year for seven years and ate one of their daughters, leaving only this last one. Now, it was coming again.

Susanoo declared that he will slay the creature if the couple give him their last daughter as his wife, to which they hastily agreed. Susanoo changes the girl into a hair comb. He secures her in his hair, then he instructes the couple on how to capture the monster: they are to distill a liquor that was refined eight times and fill eight vats with it. They must then build an encircling fence with eight gates, and they must place a vat of the liquor in front of each gate. When all is ready, they wait.

The monster appears as anticipated and is drawn to the magical elixir. It dippes one of its eight heads into each of the eight vats at the eight gates and drinks until it becomes too intoxicated to stand, whereupon it falls over and sleeps. As the creature sleeps, Susanoo hacks it to pieces with his ten-hand sword, until the river runs with blood. As he cuts the last piece of the beast's tail, his sword breaks. Surprised, Susanoo examines the tail piece and finds the mystical sword Kusanagi-no-Tsurugi inside, which becomes one of the three sacred Imperial Regalia of Japan.

Yamata-no-Orochi is an example of a *kaiju* (怪獣 "strange beast"), which evolved into a whole genre of Japanese film-making in the mid-1950s, and continues even today. Famous film kaiju include Godzilla/Gojira, Rodan, Gidorah, and Mothra. Kaiju are mythological, but don't seem to have historical roots in Japanese folklore.

❧ YŌKAI ❧

Yōkai is the general term for monsters in Japanese. Variously known as ayakashi, mononoke, or mamono, yōkai have roots in folklore, with many of them dating back centuries. Here are some yōkai types.

GASHADOKURO ARE GIGANTIC skeleton creatures that wander the countryside in search of victims to eat. When a victim is found, the Gashadokuro will seize him and bite his head off, then drain the victim of blood in an effort to flesh-out its own bony torso. These creatures are believed to be the vengeful spirits of people who have died of starvation.

JORŌGUMO HAS THE upper body of a beautiful woman and the lower body of a giant spider. She lures men to their deaths by seducing them, drawing them to isolated areas, then spinning them into bundles with her silk before draining them of blood. Some versions have the Jorōgumo stun her victims first by handing them her "baby" to hold—which then turns out to be a mass of spider eggs that explode and cover the victim with baby spiders and venom.

AKANAME ARE THE horrifying red-skinned demons of dirty bathrooms. They are described as having greasy hair, slimy skin, and long sticky tongues that they use to devour filth from uncleaned surfaces. Their most powerful ability is to spread disease.

UMIBOZO IS A giant creature of the ocean depths. It has a human shape and dark skin, but it only appears from the waist up due to the depth of the water. It will attack unsuspecting ships by swamping them with water and drowning the sailors. The only hope of escape when confronted by one of these creatures is to offer it a bottomless barrel. It is believed that the creature will repeatedly try to fill the barrel, giving the ship time to flee. The word *umibozo* is translated as "sea monk," and the creatures may be the result of vengeful monks.

ROKUROKUBI LOOK JUST like regular human females, but they have the terrifying ability to stretch their necks up to 20 feet (6 meters) in length, or worse to detach their heads altogether and let them fly about. It is said that these monsters are born human, and are transformed into evil creatures by their own bad karma or by the evil deeds of their male relatives.

JUBOKKO ARE BLOOD-SUCKING trees that are so desperate for human blood that they tear apart passing victims and consume them. Jubokko began as regular trees which happened to be located where major wars were fought; the ground was soaked with so much blood that the trees were forced to absorb it from the soil—transforming them into the wretched Jubokko. If you cut a Jubokko, it will bleed human blood.

ONI ARE JAPANESE demons or ogres with red or blue skin, wild hair, and giant stature. They carry clubs and possess numerous magical abilities, including the ability to regenerate severed body parts, shape-change, fly, spread madness and death, and cause the breakdown of society. They are also gluttons for food and drink.

⊰ YŪREI ⊱

Yūrei are the ghosts of various mythical or natural creatures. Japanese mythology is ripe with ghosts; here are some of their stories.

BAKEKUJIRA IS JAPAN'S version of *Moby Dick*. This haunted skeleton of a whale swims the coastlines at night, followed by a cadre of weird birds and unknown fish. If spotted on a foggy night, it is said that the person who saw it will have bad luck.

KASAOBAKE IS ONE of the most bizarre yūrei. It is an umbrella that became a ghost on its 100th birthday. It is said to have a single leg, one or two eyes, and a long hanging tongue. The creatures have a fondness for hunting down their former owners and eating them.

KATAKIRAUWA ARE THE ghosts of baby piglets, distinguishable from normal pigs by their odd dark skin, single ear, and glowing red eyes. It moves with a curious hopping gait, and it is believed that if the creature somehow passes between your legs, it can strip away your soul.

ONRYŌ ARE TERRIFYING vengeful spirits that arise from the souls of people who die with anger, hatred, or jealousy in their hearts. These ghosts have "unfinished business" with the living. They seek out those they feel wronged them, torturing and driving them to madness and death.

NOPPERA-BŌ ARE GHOSTS that look like humans—except they have no faces. Their name means "faceless monk," and their main occupation seems to be frightening people. They appear before their victims facing *away* from them at first, then slowly turn to reveal a ghastly visage.

INDIA

Indian civilization began some 4,500 years ago in the great Indus Valley in what is modern-day Pakistan. This civilization (or perhaps cluster of civilizations) suffered numerous invasions from northern tribes, which somehow managed to cross the shield-wall of the Himalayas. Scholars think that Hinduism arose from the roots of the belief systems of the Indus peoples somewhere during the second millennium BCE (the late Bronze Age). Hinduism may be the oldest continuously practiced religion in the world, with texts that date back to 2000 BCE and earlier. The term "Hinduism" is not without controversy; the word was coined by British writers during the Imperial period and is therefore objectionable to some. Terms such as "Vedic religion" or "hindu/sanatana dharma" may be preferable. Approximately 70 percent of the Indian population identifies themselves as Hindu, while another 10 percent identifies as Muslim. The remaining percentages are divided amongst Buddhism, Jainism, Christianity, and others.

One of the primary—if not the most important—tenets of Hinduism is truth. But Hindus don't believe that truth is didactic. Instead, truth can be found in many places and all truth is relative to the place, time, and culture of whomever espouses it. Therefore, modern Hindus believe strongly in the need for tolerance and the broad-based search for knowledge from disparate sources.

This belief in the relativity of truth has led, in part, to the development of the massive pantheon of Hindu gods and goddesses, and the wealth of mythology, doctrine, and practice that accompanies it. Reincarnation (or, more properly, "transmigration") is a central belief of Hinduism, particularly in Southeast Asia. The soul or spirit is believed to be reborn into another form after death; which form the soul takes in the next life is dependent upon the *karma*—determined by the good or bad actions a person did in previous lives—of the person who died.

HINDU GODS AND GODDESSES

It is said that there are two million gods and goddesses in the Hindu pantheon, and that they are *all* worshipped. A number of these deities are avatars of some of the primary immortals, while others could be considered lesser gods that may appear sporadically or in special circumstances. Here are some of the gods and goddesses of Hindu mythology.

⚐ AGNI ⚐

Agni is the fire god, friend and protector of humanity, and guardian of the home; more hymns in the Vedas are offered to Agni than any other deity. The parents of Agni are variously listed as Aditi and Kashyapa/Kasyapa, Dyaus (the Vedic sky father) and Prithvi/Prithivi, or even Lord Brahma himself.

⚐ GANESH/GANESHA ⚐

The elephant-headed son of Shiva and Parvati, Ganesh is the lord of intellect and wisdom and god of good fortune and overcoming obstacles—which is demonstrated by his single tusk. He is usually depicted as having red or yellow skin and the body of a man, in addition to his elephant head—which he received from Shiva after the Destroyer lopped off the youngster's human head in a fit of anger. He also has a large body and four arms (which represent his divinity); he is the embodiment of the primordial sound "OM," from whence all hymns arose. Ganesh has three wives, and he also represents the perfect balance between kindness and strength, power and beauty, truth and illusion, the real and the unreal. Ganesh rides upon a mouse, which represents ignorance and his dominion over it.

⚜ KALI ⚜

Kali is the Dark Mother. The terrifying avatar of Shakti, Kali represents the ferocity of motherly love. She typically has blue or black skin, four (or frequently eight to ten) arms, a long protruding tongue, red eyes, and a face and chest caked with blood. Each of her hands holds a fearsome weapon, usually a sword of some type. Her earrings are severed human heads and a necklace of fifty heads (each representing a letter of the Sanskrit alphabet) encircles her neck; her skirt is made from severed human arms and hands. She may be shown standing on the body of her husband, Shiva, who threw himself beneath her feet to stop her murderous rampage. She has three eyes in order to see the past, present, and future (kala is the Sanskrit word for "time"). Kali's worshipers have a deep relationship with the goddess, and are said to love her like their own mothers.

⚜ LAKSHMI ⚜

Goddess of beauty and light, good fortune and wealth, Lakshmi is the wife and Shakti (sacred energy) of Vishnu, and she reincarnates with him each time he takes the form of one of his avatars: she is Sita to his Rama, and Radha and Rukmini to his Krishna. Lakshmi is depicted as a beautiful fair-skinned woman with four arms (an indication of divinity), standing or sitting upon a *padma* (the sacred lotus). She is often accompanied by one or two elephants who shower the waters of the ocean upon her. She was elevated from the Milky Sea by the primeval war god Indra, who churned the sea with the help of the other gods to raise the world's treasures from its depths. Lakshmi is rarely without Vishnu, and may frequently be found massaging the feet of the protector god. Lakshmi is the influence for goddesses of a number of other nations, including Vadsudhara in Nepal and the Tibet Region of China, Dewi Sri in Bali (Indonesia), and Kishijoten in Japan. Lakshmi rides upon an owl.

⊰ Parjana/Parjanya ⊱

God of rain, thunderstorms, lightning, and monsoons, Parjana has dominion over the reproduction of all vegetation and living creatures, though there is debate as to whether he was originally the god of rain or the god of thunder. He is compared to the Lithuanian thunder god, Perkūnas, and the Norse god, Thor. Parjanya is the husband of Prithvi (also Bhūmi), who is the embodiment of the earth and the sacred cow Vasa, whose milk represents the life-giving rain. He is associated with the Vedic Lord Varuna (the sky god) as a cloud deity. Parjanya appears as a fair-skinned man with four arms, who is seated on a lotus blossom. He wears gold earrings and a large gold crown with a gold circlet and a rainbow halo behind it; he often holds lotus flowers in two of his hands. He is also one of the twelve Adityas—the children of Aditi, goddess of the sky and mother of the gods. Suraya (the sun) is primary among the Adityas, which can be compared to the zodiac signs of Western astrology. The Adityas each shine in a different month of the year; Parjanya's is the month of Kártik.

⊰ Parvati ⊱

In addition to being the wife of Shiva, Parvati is also the *shakti* (or life energy) that produced the gods Ganesha, Karitkeya (god of war), and Ashokasundari (goddess of imagination). Parvati is the Mother Goddess in Hindu religion; she has dominion over fertility, marriage, love, beauty, children, and devotion (especially marital fidelity). Kali is a terrifying aspect of Parvati—representing maternal love. Parvati is the model for Tara in Chinese and Nepalese Buddhism, Cybele in Greco-Roman mythology, and the Greek goddess

Vesta. She is the nurturing aspect of the supreme Hindu goddess Devi. Together with Lakshmi and Saraswati, Parvati forms the Tridevi—the holy trinity of the goddess, which complements and assists the Trimurti in the business of creating, maintaining, and recycling the universe. Parvati rides upon Dawon, the lion.

⚜ SARASWATI ⚜

Saraswati is the wife of Brahma and goddess of knowledge, learning, wisdom, and the arts. She is shakti to the creator god and forms part of the Tridevi. She is the origin of the goddess Anahita in ancient Persia, Athena/Minerva in ancient Greece and Rome, and Benzaiten (弁財天) in Japan. She is the sister of Shiva the Destroyer, and she rides either a swan or a peacock.

⚜ SURYA ⚜

The sun and the sun god, Surya is the first-born son of Aditi (the mother of gods) and her husband Kashyapa, a revered Vedic sage. Surya drives a golden chariot pulled by seven white horses across the sky (predating Apollo and Sól).

HINDU MYTHICAL MONSTERS

As there are legions of gods, so there are legions of monsters as well. Here are a few of the monsters of Hindu myth.

⚜ ALMAS/ALMA ⚜
MONGOLIA

Essentially a Mongolian Bigfoot, Almas is a humanoid covered with hair and unable to speak. It converses in grunts and is also found in Chechen, Turkish, and Russian myth. It inhabits the Caucasus and Altai mountains in this region. The Chinese version is the Yeren, the Indian is the Mande Barung, the Sumatran is the Orang Pendek, the Pakistani is the Barmanou, and the Nepali is the Meh-teh. The Americas have Bigfoot.

⊰ APSONSI ⊱
THAI

Apsonsi is a half-woman, half-lion creature (also Apsarasingha, and other spellings) that lives in the legendary Himavanta forest in the Himalayas. Believed to be protectors from harm, they frequently stand guard at Buddhist temples.

⊰ KALA ⊱
HINDU

A monster that is the personification of time, the *kala* is an aspect of the destroyer god, Shiva. It is also considered to be one of the primary forms of Vishnu in the *Vishnu Purana*. Kala is the messenger of Yama, god of death. Batara Kala is the god of destruction in Javanese mythology, and is portrayed as a huge and powerful giant.

⊰ KALAVIṄKA ⊱
BUDDHIST

Kalaviṅka is an immortal creature with a human head on a bird's body and a long, flowing tail. It sings while still in the egg with a beautiful voice, which is said to emulate the voice of Buddha. It is similar to the Korean *Inmyeonjo*.

⊰ KINNARA ⊱
HINDU

With a top half that is human and bottom half that is horse, Kinnara is a celestial musician. In Southeast Asia, the Kinnara (male) and Kinnari (female) are cherished, benevolent deities that are half human and half bird. They live in the Himalayas, and fly over humanity in troubled times, keeping the people safe. The Kinnaris are renowned singers, dancers, and poets; they symbolize the feminine attributes of beauty, grace, and skill in the arts.

⊰ KIRTIMUKHA ⊱
HINDU

Kirtimukha is a fearsome monster with enormous fangs and a huge, gaping mouth. It is a motif, found on buildings and ornamental art, rather than a mythical monster. Its name means "glory face," and it represents greed; it is an archetype referred to as a "swallowing god." A similar motif is Simhamuka (a lion face).

⊰ MAKARA ⊱
HINDU

The vehicle (*vahana*) of the goddess Ganga and the sea god Varuna, the Makara is the front half of a land animal (usually a deer or elephant) with the back half of a fish or seal, sometimes a snake or even a flower. It is the Hindu astrological equivalent of the sign of Capricorn in the Western zodiac. Makara (singular and plural) guard temple entrances, and are used as motifs by a number of other Hindu gods, including Shiva and Surya. Makara's personality is that of a crocodile.

⊰ MONGOLIAN DEATH WORM ⊱
MONGOLIA

This is a giant worm about 5 feet (1.5 meters) long that looks like a big, red strand of cow gut. It spits acid at those who approach it, and if you foolishly touch it, you will die instantly.

⊰ PENANGGALAN ⊱
MALAYSIA

A horrifying monster with a taste for newborn babies (human babies), this creature appears as a normal woman during the daytime, but come nightfall its head pops off and flies about searching for victims, especially pregnant women. It drags its human entrails behind it as it flies, and then must clean them with vinegar and reinsert them into its body by sunrise. The smell of vinegar surrounds it.

⊰ PHAYA NAGA ⊱
LAOS

Phaya Naga is a benign water dragon that lives in the Mekong River and guards the cities along it. Phaya Naga can shoot fireballs from its mouth and is also known in Cambodia, Vietnam, Burma, and Thailand.

⚐ Shesha/Shesahnaga/Adishesha ⚑
Hindu

The king of all serpents and servant of Vishnu, Shesha is one of the original, primal beings of the universe. The Puranas describe him as holding the objects of the universe on his one thousand hoods, and singing the praises of Vishnu from his one thousand mouths. Shesha floats coiled in the void of space, or sometimes on the primordial ocean. As Shesha spreads his coils, time moves forward. When he begins to coil up again, time and the universe will be exterminated. *Shesha* means "that which remains."

⚐ Vetala ⚑
India

Essentially vampires, these are dead people who walk the earth because the proper funeral rites were not performed over them. They could also be evil spirits that inhabit and animate corpses. Recognizable by its backwards hands and feet, a Vetal (singular) can see forward and backward in time, and use that knowledge to confuse its victims. Vetala can be enslaved to act as guards or assistants for sorcerers, and they have been known to kill children and domestic animals.

HINDU SUPERSTITIONS

Given the enormous variety of deities and the numerous tribes that make up the peoples of India, it isn't surprising that a great number of superstitions have risen there.

HANGING A LEMON strung with exactly seven hot chilis (called a *nimbu totka*) is believed to deter evil spirits, as well as Alakshmi, god of misfortune. There seems to be some basis for the effectiveness of this tradition: citrus and chilis both contain high amounts of vitamin C, and allegedly, the vitamin is absorbed by the cotton string that runs through the fruits when they are strung and is then released back into the air. Vitamin C is proven to have benefits in promoting lung and immune system health. Also, the odor of citrus can repel insects and other pests (this is how citronella candles work).

TAKE A BATH after attending a funeral. This one makes good sense. Decomposing bodies release a number of toxins and bacteria into the air, which may contaminate mourners.

THROW COINS INTO fountains and holy bodies of water. Historically, many coins contained significant amounts of copper (a metallic element with high chemical reactivity). The copper acted as a chemical treatment in water supplies, making them safer for people to consume by killing bacteria and providing a necessary element for health. Throwing coins into wells and fountains is a tradition that has become associated with luck the world over.

AVOID CUTTING/TRIMMING YOUR hair and fingernails on Saturday. It is believed that doing so will anger the planet Saturn (Shani) and bring bad luck. Apparently, planets have a will of their own that we knew nothing about. Black cats are also bad luck because black is the color of Shani.

AVOID THE NUMBER eight. Again, Shani rules the number eight and everything associated with Shani appears to be unlucky!

KEEP ONIONS (AND KNIVES!) under your bed to prevent bad dreams. This is commonly done under baby cribs, so that the child sleeps peacefully. If the nightmare monster is not driven away by the smell, perhaps you are supposed to stab it to death? Curiously, putting an onion under your pillow is supposed to bring dreams of your future love partner.

SHAKING YOUR LEGS will drive away your wealth. Maybe because you'll jingle your change out through that hole in your pocket?

DON'T SWEEP THE floor in the evening or you will sweep Lakshmi right out the door. It is said that this goddess likes to visit homes in the evening (particularly between the hours of 6 and 7p.m.), and that sweeping will prevent her from entering the home.

CROW DUNG IS lucky. A number of animals are sacred in Hinduism, and spotting crow crap is said to mean that money is coming to you. The word for this bonus in Hindi is *laabh*; Labh is one of the sons of Ganesh, the Hindu god of good fortune.

ADD ONE RUPEE for luck. When gifting money, be sure the amount ends in "one;" odd numbers are said to be better than even numbers, and the number one is particularly lucky.

FLAT FEET ARE unlucky. Indian mothers-in-law may check to see if the bride-to-be has flat feet because it is believed that a woman with flat feet will become a widow.

KOHL PROTECTS AGAINST the evil eye. The Indian concept of the evil eye is referred to as *buri nazar*, and means that for every good thing that happens, something bad is likely to follow. Putting a *tikka* (spot) of kohl on a baby forehead and/or cheek is said to prevent buri nazar.

TO PREVENT CARDIOVASCULAR disease, make sure the head of your bed does *not* face north. This has to do with earth's electromagnetic fields.

CRUSH THE HEAD of a snake after killing it, lest the severed head bites you. Believe it or not, this is fact. According to *National Geographic*, snakes have reflex muscles that can remain active up to an hour after the head is severed and the snake is officially "dead." The head can bite and inject venom in that time period!

PLASTERING THE FLOOR with cow dung is lucky. Cows are sacred in India, and everything connected to cows is considered auspicious. It is said that the dung also repels insects and reptiles—helpful, since there are a lot of those in India. This practice began before the advent of modern chemical cleaners, and still continues in parts of the country.

Note: A word about *sati* (also *suttee*): this notorious practice that involves burning alive the widow or mistress of a deceased man on the same funeral pyre as the deceased was officially outlawed on January 3, 1988, due to an incident that occurred the previous year. Although the practice is banned by law, it does still occur.

THE AMERICAS

Historical civilizations in the Americas derive directly from Asia. People migrated into North and South America from the Asian continent at the end of the last Ice Age, both by walking across a land bridge in the Bering Sea and by boat. The boats then took them down the western American coast from what's now Alaska all the way to Patagonia. Because of their physical isolation, civilizations in the Americas remained "primitive" as the rest of the world entered the Iron Age. This didn't stop American civilizations from developing rich cultural and political traditions as well as intriguing mythologies.

This section will examine the stories of the Americas by regions starting with North America (Canada and the United States) followed by Mexico and Central America, and then ending with South America. Along the way, the fascinating folklore and mythologies of the regions' First Nations and Native American cultures and peoples will be presented. There are numerous possessions and territories in and around these regions that belong to countries from outside the region (e.g. Greenland belongs to Denmark, the Virgin Islands are split between Britain and the US), but for simplicity's sake, we'll examine them in the context of their geography.

Putting Inuit lands (e.g. Alaska) with Canada, rather than with the US, may seem confusing; however, the traditions of the indigenous peoples of Alaska do not match those of native peoples of the continental US for the most part. Native Americans, or First Nations, are descended from the group of people who crossed the theorized land bridge from Eastern Russia and Asia to North America about twenty thousand years ago. Some of their mythologies have details in common with those of native Alaskans.

CANADA

Canadian culture has been influenced by conquest, mainly from Britain and France, but also by immigration as well as its own indigenous peoples. When we look at the myths and legends of Canada, we find that some are directly taken from indigenous folklore and religion, while others might be a blend of indigenous and European lore. Here are some of the great myths and legends of Canada.

CANADIAN MONSTERS AND LEGENDS

A number of the legends of this area refer to inanimate rather than animate objects.

⊰ CHASSE-GALERIE ⊱
FRENCH FOLKTALE

This weird legend concerns a group of undefined people who need to cover a great distance in a short period of time. They decide to make a pact with Satan (!), who turns their canoe into a speed-flying boat. Satan instructs them that they can go wherever they wish in the boat—but they must not utter the name Jesus Christ, lest Satan claim their souls. Along the way, however, the group members get royally drunk, and one of them starts spouting the names of God and Jesus. The others try to stop him, but the flying boat crashes to earth, rendering them all senseless. When they regain consciousness, they discover that they are all in Hell. The title *Chasse-galerie* is generally accepted to mean "flying canoe" or "bewitched canoe," though its precise translation is more like "bewitched hunt."

⇥ Cressie ⇤
Newfoundland

This 15-foot (4.5-meter) monster is said to inhabit the waters of Crescent Lake, located in Roberts Arm, Newfoundland. The tiny town (population about 840) has recorded numerous sightings of the creature, some dating back to its earliest days and tribal legends. The monster is said to be serpent-like and to live in the deepest parts of the lake. Oh, and it also has the ability to shape-shift.

⇥ Dancing with the Devil, ⇤
also The Legend of Rose Latulippe
European Folktale

There are dozens of versions of this story, but basically a young and foolish girl chooses to dance with a stranger until midnight. When the hour strikes, the stranger reveals himself to be none other than Satan himself. The girl is terrified, but it is too late to escape. Satan kidnaps her and takes her down to Hell, where she remains to this day. Moral? Don't dance with strangers!

⇥ Dungarvon Whooper ⇤
New Brunswick

This bizarre tale is told amongst the lumberjacks and woodsmen of the Dungarvon River basin in New Brunswick. It seems that there was once a cook's helper, a young boy who worked in a lumber camp along the river. Inexplicably, the camp boss killed, cooked, and ate the boy one day. The boss told the lumbermen that the boy had run away. That night, the camp was shaken by unearthly screams; the lumbermen abandoned the camp in terror the next day. The boy's ghost is said to haunt that site to this very day.

⚔ THE FORBIDDEN PLATEAU ⚔
BRITISH COLUMBIA

Within the hills of British Columbia lies a wooded, hilly plateau dotted with small lakes. Once home to the K'omoks/Comox people, the rugged area was used as a safe haven for the families of tribal members during hostile raids by coastal tribes. It is said that long ago the families were hidden there as usual, but when the men returned to the area to collect their wives and children after another raid, no trace of the families could be found. The area was deemed to be the home of evil spirits who had taken the families and was declared to be off limits. In 1946, the most powerful earthquake ever recorded on land in Canada—a mighty 7.3 on the Richter scale—hit the plateau, and fortunately damage and loss of life were minimal.

⚔ GHOST SHIP TEAZER ⚔
NOVA SCOTIA

Here's a great tale of a (supposedly real) ship. The ship *Young Teazer* was a schooner that was sunk during the War of 1812 off the coast of Nova Scotia. People believe it can still be seen—glowing with fire—sailing through the mists of morning. Making the tale even more interesting is the detail that *Young Teazer* was a licensed pirate ship—a rare and juicy tidbit in ghost-ship lore.

⚔ GHOST SHIP (II) ⚔
PRINCE EDWARD ISLAND AND NORTHUMBERLAND

The Ghost Ship of Northumberland Strait has the distinction of being Canada's best-known haunted ship. Sightings have been recorded for over two hundred years, and usually tell of a three-masted ship that bursts into flame when other vessels try to approach it. As the rescue ships come closer, the mysterious schooner disappears. The name and origin of the ship are unknown.

⚔ GHOST TRAIN ⚔
QUEBEC

Saskatchewan is home to the regional legend of the Ghost Train. The legend centers around the small town of St. Louis, where an abandoned railroad track lies. Strange lights can be seen moving along the tracks on certain nights. The lights are attributed to the Ghost Train, or to the ghost of a deceased railway worker.

⚔ Oak Island Money Pit ⚔
Nova Scotia

This is the legend familiar to audiences worldwide, and the basis for a popular TV show. Oak Island exists off the coast of Nova Scotia, and is home to the mysterious "money pit:" a 230-foot (70-meter) deep hole that was dug by parties unknown and laden with numerous "booby traps," consisting of falling platforms, water traps, and false floors. The pit has been worked for over 150 years by various individuals and financially-backed groups, resulting in the deaths of six treasure hunters (part of the legend stipulates that the treasure will not be found until seven people have died looking for it). A second legend states that as long as there are oak trees on the island, the treasure will not be found. To date, there is still one oak tree left. A number of theories about the pit have been put forth in recent years, most based on the small objects recovered from various digs. Whether it's the remains of a Viking fishing camp, or the ultimate guardian of pirate booty, no one knows.

Inuit/First Nations

Though we are looking at these two groups together, they are *not* the same: Inuit are the peoples formerly called "Eskimos," who traditionally lived on the islands and along the coasts of far northern Canada and what is now Alaska. First Nations are native peoples who lived in the lands between the Pacific and the Atlantic Oceans *below* the Arctic Circle. A third group is recognized in Canada: the Métis. These people are descended from First Nations people who joined with Europeans. There are a number of different Inuit groups: Caribou Inuit, Copper Inuit, Netsilik Inuit, Inuit at Amitsoq Lake, and Iglulik Inuit, to name a few. The mythologies and culture of each of these groups is somewhat different, thus some of the gods and goddesses, and the stories about them, will be different as well. The various beings and tales in this book are representative of different Inuit groups.

INUIT GODS AND GODDESSES

Inuit mythology draws heavily from the sea-going lifestyle of the people. This is a good way to differentiate it from the myths of the land-based First Nations.

⊰ KINAK ⊱

Kinak is the mountain-sized god of the north wind, and son of the breath of life, Sila. His freezing breath could kill, and his enormous reclining body comprised an entire mountain range. One legend tells of a human woman named Taku who fled her wife-beating husband and took refuge in the mountains that were Kinak. The wind god took pity after hearing her story and allowed her to live on him for many years. Eventually, Kinak needed to shift his position onto his other side, which meant that Taku had to return home. Kinak sent her with a load of valuable furs that made her and her husband very rich. For a time, the couple were happy and even had a son, but Taku's husband took up his old ways and began beating her again. She prayed to Kinak, who used his killing breath to blow the husband far, far away, and he was never seen again. Taku's son became a great hunter, but unfortunately he inherited his father's evil temperament. When the son began killing competing hunters, Kinak eventually blew him away, too.

⊰ NANUQ/NANOOK ⊱

Nanuq is the Inuit word for "polar bear"; it is also sometimes listed as the Master of Bears, or as the god of polar bears.

⊰ Nunam ⊱

As goddess of the earth, Nunam is sometimes considered the wife of Sila. She wears a long coat from which dangle living miniature versions of the land creatures she created (with the exception of caribou); she has fur boots and fur bracelets as well. It is said that in her early days, Nunam bore the children of men as flowers upon her surface; Inuit women gained children by plucking the flowers. The precious musk-oxen were believed to hatch from large eggs planted deep in Nunam's earthly body. Before time began, Sila came down from the heavens and coupled with Nunam, producing the first man (named Kallak). Nunam then coupled with Kallak to produce the first woman; Kallak then took the first woman as his wife, and the two of them populated the earth with humans.

⊰ Pukimna/Pinga/Caribou Mother ⊱

Pukimna, the goddess of the caribou, lived an isolated life surrounded by huge herds of caribou, which she created from her trousers and which were under her control. When man violated her taboos, Pukimna would keep the herds away from them so hunters could not find food. She is also credited with creating the souls of walruses (which seem like they should have been under Sedna's purview), and for likewise keeping the walruses away from non-observant hunters. Pukimna created the walruses from her boots. Originally, Pukimna's caribou had tusks like the walrus, but these made them too dangerous for men to hunt, so she turned the tusks into antlers. The animals still ran too fast for the hunters, so Pukimna slowed them down by roughing up the hair on the bellies, flanks, and throats of the beasts to make them less aerodynamic. Finally, she kicked them in the head, leaving a dent in their foreheads that they retain even today.

⊰ Sedna ⊱

This sea goddess, or goddess of the sea mammals, may be the most revered deity in Inuit mythology. She is the daughter of Anguta (god of a coastal island) and Isarrataitsoq (with whom Sedna would come to share the giant scorpion god Kanajuk as husband). The legend of Sedna says that she was so hungry she devoured both of her mother's arms and one of her father's arms before Anguta was able to subdue her and take her out to sea in a canoe. There, he threw her overboard with the intent of abandoning her; Sedna, however, clung to the side of the canoe with her hands. Desperate, Anguta chopped off her fingers with his knife, sending her to the briny depths. There, Sedna transformed her fingerless hands into flippers while the fingers themselves became the great animals of the sea.

Anguta, still with just one arm, paddled back to shore and his waiting, armless wife. Sedna, now transformed into the goddess of the sea (but still mad about being abandoned), splashed a giant wave over her parents, which swept them from the shore and into the abyss of the sea. Sedna then forced them into service in her underwater court. Anguta would serve as judge of the souls of the dead, punishing them for taboos they had broken in life. When the punishment was considered justly served, the souls were free to go to the land of the dead, called Adlivun, where they existed happily while awaiting reincarnation.

⇥ Seqinek ⇤

The sun goddess, Seqinek, holds her blazing
torch (the sun) aloft as she runs across the
daytime sky to escape her lecherous brother,
the moon god Tatqimt. He is far behind
her, bearing his half-extinguished torch
(the moon) through the dark skies of night.
Seqinek reaches their shared home at dusk,
entering just after Tatqimt has left for his
nightly pursuit; the two of them are never in
the home at the same time.

⇥ Sila/Silla/Silap Inua/ Hilap Inua/Hilla ⇤

Sila is the god of the sky, weather, and the wind (considered the animating life
force of creation). Wind was thought of as "the breath of the world," casting Sila
as deity of human and animal breathing. The life force flowed from Sila at birth
and back to Sila at death. Since singing, storytelling, and humming all require the
breath, Sila also oversees those things, as well as creative inspiration. The whispers
of intuition are said to be from Sila; the nagging of conscience is also attributed to
Sila. He creates snow by letting his ivory shavings fall the earth as he carves. He is
depicted as being clean-shaven and bare-chested to the freezing weather he creates.

⚞ TAPASUMA ⚟

Tapasuma is the goddess of the celestial afterlife (counterpart to Sedna, who rules the aquatic afterlife). The two afterlives are a result of location of the groups espousing them: coastal Inuits hold with the underwater afterlife of Sedna (Adlivun), while intercontinental Inuits believe in Tapasuma's celestial realm (Udlormiat, the land of perpetual daylight). In both, punishments and rewards depend on the successful observance of various taboos during a soul's life. The earth is seen as a giant igloo, and the stars are said to be holes in the roof of the igloo where light from Udlormiat come through. Souls in Udlormiat have plenty of food, warmth, and leisure time—much of it spent playing the Inuit version of soccer. The aurora borealis is said to be the souls moving back and forth on the playing field. When at last the souls grow bored with Udlormiat, they present themselves to Tapasuma to be reincarnated on earth.

⚞ TATQIMT/TARQEQ/TARQIUP INUA ⚟

The moon god Tatqimt carries his partially-lit torch (the moon) as he lustfully chases his sister Seqinek, whose fully-lit torch is the sun. Tatqimt is important to the cycle of reincarnation: as the souls of the dead are ready to leave Udlormiut to be reincarnated, the goddess Tapasuma bids Tatqimt to take the souls back to earth and gives him instructions regarding what form each soul is to be reincarnated. In his giant dogsled pulled by four enormous (or just one *really* enormous) dogs, Tatqimt transports the souls to earth on moonless nights (which accounts for why the moon is absent from the sky during those few days each month). Tatqimt also controls the tides (vital to Inuit life) and oversees hunting, making him perhaps the most important god in the Inuit pantheon.

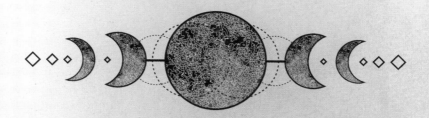

INUIT MYTHICAL MONSTERS

As in the previous section, monsters of the Inuit often have ocean connections, too.

⊰ ADLET/ERQIGDLIT ⊱

Said to be the result of a human woman having relations with a wolf (or sometimes a huge dog), the Adlet are essentially werewolves. The legend says that the woman gave birth to ten children: five were wolves and five were Adlet. The Adlet had the upper torso of a man and the lower torso of a wolf. Terrified, the woman set the Adlet adrift on the open sea. Instead of perishing, the five managed to travel to Europe, where they became the progenitors of European werewolves. The five which remained with the woman grew into man-eating canine hominids (pseudo-humans), which wander the earth looking for the unwary to feast upon.

⊰ AKHLUT ⊱

This bizarre creature is portrayed as a cross between a killer whale (orca) and a wolf. The presence of wolf tracks that lead to the ocean is a sign of the creature's presence. The Akhlut is a shape-shifter with the ability to hunt on the land or in the sea. It is quite vicious, and it will attack people trying to drag fish from the sea, as well as people who sleep too close to the shore. Another name for orca is "seawolf."

⊨ AMAROK/AMAROQ ⊨

Sometimes referred to as the "wolf god," Amarok is the primordial wolf—the first wolf on earth. He is much larger than normal wolves, and he hunts alone instead of in packs. A tale of Amarok has a man floating his boat (or paddling a kayak) down a river. He comes upon a litter of wolf pups and, in a drunken spree, kills them all. Suddenly, a huge wolf (sometimes described as the mother, sometimes as Amarok) leaps from the bushes and bites the man's stomach, wrenching his soul from the flesh. Dazed, the man returns to his village and his people, only to be shunned by them because he has no soul. In some traditions, Amaguq (name slightly different) is a trickster wolf-god.

⊨ A-MI-KUK/AH-MIN-KUK ⊨

This monster has moist, slick skin, and—instead of legs—the arms and hands of humans, which it uses to walk upon the land. It is huge and heavy, and will attack and eat anyone foolish enough to bathe in the ocean. It also eats enormous quantities of fish.

⊨ KEELUT/KE'LETS/QIQION/QIQIRN ⊨

Keelut is a subterranean beast that resembles a black, hairless dog which feeds upon the dead. The only hair is on the creature's feet, which serves to mask and/or erase its tracks so no one can see its comings and goings. The creature stalks the unwary, and it is considered to be a harbinger of death.

⚜ QALUPALIK ⚜

Qalupalik is a monster of the sea who lures little children to their deaths by humming. She has green skin, long hair, and very long fingernails; she wears a traditional *amautik*—a parka made especially for women—which has a pouch in the back of it just below the hood for a woman to carry her baby against her back to keep it warm. When a child draws close to the shoreline, the Qalupalik will leap onshore, grab the child, and tuck it into her amautik—never to see its family again.

⚜ TIZHERUK ⚜

These are large sea serpents with 7-foot (2.1-meter)-long heads atop 15-foot (4.5-meter)-long bodies. Their bodies end in a flipper, and they are said to grab unsuspecting people from docks and piers. (Some have humorously suggested that the Tizheruk were invented to cover up peoples' clumsiness around icy surfaces). The Tizheruk share some features with the Haietlik, or "Lightning Snakes," sometimes associated with the Thunderbird of the Pacific Northwest tribes. The Thunderbird is said to use the Haietlik as weapons when hunting orcas—throwing the Haietlik like lightning bolts down upon the orcas.

⚔ TORNITS/ALASKA BUSHMEN ⚔

Tornits are allegedly aboriginal peoples who lived in Alaska before the Inuit crossed the Bering Sea. Originally, the Inuit and the Tornits were able to live side by side in peace and to share hunting grounds. The Inuit made kayaks to help themselves hunt—a skill that the Tornits were apparently unable to master, but the advantages of which they understood very well. Legend tells of a young Tornit who "borrowed" the kayak of an Inuit without permission and subsequently damaged it. Enraged, the Inuit stabbed the Tornit in the neck, killing him. The remaining Tornits fled into the Alaskan wilderness in fear for their lives, lest the Inuits decide to kill them all. Ever since, tales of hunters who go missing only to turn up dead and/or mangled in the brush circulate through the hunting camps. Beware of the revenge of the Tornits!

⚔ TUPILAQ ⚔

These are demonic figures carved from organic materials (whale bone, walrus tusk, wood, etc.) that are cursed to life by witches and evil shamen—similar to the Golem from Jewish folklore. The figures are then set in the sea to kill a specific person. The success or failure of the Tupilaq's mission depends on the relative strength of the witch's powers; if the target person is more powerful than the witch, the Tupilaq could be sent back to kill the witch instead. Different Inuit cultures have different meanings for the Tupilaq: in some, it is an invisible ghost of a dead person that only a shaman can see, while others say that it is a chimera consisting of a human head attached to parts from various animals. In such cases, the Tupilaq—whether ghost or chimera—can attack Inuit settlements and has to be dealt with by the shaman. Tupilaq can be compared to Tokoloshe/Tikoloshe from Zulu (African) mythology and Anchimayen (also Anchimallén or Anchimalguén, in Spanish) from Mapuche (Chile) mythology.

INUIT TABOOS

Bad luck hunting, suffering as a spirit in the afterlife, or coming face-to-face with some of the many monsters in Inuit mythology was often the result of some poor unfortunate person having broken a taboo. Taboos are vital in the harsh conditions of the Arctic; some taboos are in place for good reason, some just seem curious today. A few of the cultural taboos of the Inuit are as follows.

WEAPONS USED FOR hunting land animals have to be purified by smoke from a seaweed fire before being used to hunt sea animals.

CLOTHING FROM CARIBOU hide cannot be sewn while seals are being hunted—and vice versa.

SEA ANIMALS AND land animals can not be eaten on the same day.

SICK PEOPLE AND women who are about to give birth have to be separated from other people. The woman stays in a separate house for a month, avoiding certain forbidden foods and not leaving the house to go visiting.

AFTER BIRTH, THE child's umbilical cord is either bitten or cut off with a sharp mussel shell and then saved as a powerful amulet for the child. Many amulets are worn to avert evil or ensure good luck: owl claws are made for strong hands; caribou ears give acute hearing; willow branches ensure growth. Tattoos are given to women to protect them from evil spirits and ensure that they have a happy afterlife.

CHILDREN ARE OFTEN named after a dead relative (or several dead relatives) in the hope that the stronger spirit of the deceased adult will protect the weak spirit of the child until it grows up.

THE DEAD ARE wrapped in skins and laid upon the tundra or in the hills, inside a ring of stones. The family of the deceased must bathe themselves and clean the house after the burial.

UNITED STATES

The US began as a cluster of colonies belonging to England. Before the land could be fully explored, the French and the Spanish had claimed huge tracts of the New World for themselves. Tens of millions of settlers poured into and then spread across the vast "undiscovered" lands—only to run up hard against the people who had been living there for millennia. People who had uprooted their lives and sold everything for a chance at a new life in the States were very unhappy at the notion of having to share "their" land with indigenous peoples—particularly when those peoples were considered "savages." Within the span of a couple of hundred years, the native population had been all but wiped off the face of the earth. The survivors were pushed onto "reservations" (as though these lands were a special gift from the government) and essentially left to wither away from disease and starvation.

NATIVE AMERICANS

The history of the indigenous peoples of the Americas did not begin with the arrival of the first Europeans. It began, instead, about sixteen thousand years ago, when the last Ice Age first relented and the great glacial sheets that covered much of North America began to melt. Current genetic research indicates that a small group of people from the far eastern point of Russia began moving across the Bering Strait to the new lands of the Americas as the ice receded. Though we aren't sure exactly when the Russian migrants arrived in the Americas, it is generally agreed upon that between about 10,000 to 8,000 BCE the inhabitants were transitioning from hunter-gatherers to a more agricultural way of life. They developed more permanent settlements, and perfected the arts of pottery, loom weaving, and animal husbandry. With advances in civilization and less time spent following the grazing herds, came a bit more leisure time and the pursuits of arts such as storytelling, music, and religion.

Despite the evidence that indigenous peoples are descended from a common ancestral group (except the Native Alaskans, who arrived in a much later migration), the mythology and folklore of these people varies considerably by geography. Similarities in artistic style and illustration can be seen in Pacific coastal and South American groups (such as the Inca), but mythology was impacted by the tribes' differing climate and way of life. North American Subarctic peoples can be broadly separated into two distinct groups: Algonquin-speaking tribes of the eastern continent, such as the Algonquin, Cree, Innu, and Ojibwa, and Athabaskan-speaking tribes of the western continent such as the Chipewyan, Hupa, and Tolowa. Southwestern native languages such as Western Apache and Navajo are also Athabaskan.

NATIVE AMERICAN GODS AND GODDESSES OF SOUTHWEST TRIBES

It is helpful to examine the myths of Native Americans in relation to the geography of the tribes.

⊰ DIYIN DINE'É ⊱

Diyin Dine'é are the "Holy People" of Navaho legend. Not described as "gods," per se, but more like immortal beings, the Diyin Dine'é created the sun, the moon, the stars, and the constellations. The names of the Holy People are as follows.

HAASHCH'ÉÉLTI'Í (Talking God): His body is white, and he's from the Third World.

TÓ NEINILÍ (Water Sprinkler): His body is blue. He is ruler of the rain and from the Third World.

HAASHCH'ÉÉ'OOGHAAN (House God): His body is yellow. He's from the Third World.

HAASHCH'ÉÉSHZHINÍ (or the Black Yé'ii): This ruler of fire helped change Turquoise Boy into the sun and is from the Third World.

MA'IITO'Í ÁLCHÍNÍ (Great Coyote Who Was Formed In Water): This is one One of the original first four Holy People from the First World.

Áltsé Hashké (Coyote-Called-First-Angry): This is one of the original first four Holy People from the First World.

Áltsé hastiin (First Man): His is one One of the original first four Holy People from the First World.

Áltsé asdzaá (First Woman): She is one of the original first four Holy People from the First World.

Kachina (English)/ katsina (Hopi)/ Kököle (Zuni)

Kachina are spirit beings (similar to totems in other native cultures) which embody certain aspects of life among the Pueblo tribes of the Southwest US (especially the Hopi and the Zuni). Each kachina has three aspects: the spirit itself, the kachina dancers, and the kachina dolls. The dolls are believed to actually house the spirit beings, so the dolls are only given to those who are believed to be capable of caring for the spirit and giving it the respect it is due. The dolls are extremely popular as tourist items, but the tribes to which they are sacred will not sell them. Other tribes in the region (notably the Navaho) have taken to creating copies of the dolls, which are then sold to tourists. Kachina dancers are understood to be the temporary embodiment of the spirits themselves, and they make their appearances only on special occasions.

⊰ Wuya ⊱

Wuya are the most important of the Hopi kachina. They rank higher in the hierarchy of spirits, and they typically represent the more vital aspects of Pueblo culture. Here are some of the Wuya.

Ahul: spirit of the sky and the sun.

Alosaka: spirit of crop growth (usually seen as a pair with Muyingua, spirit of seed germination).

Angak: spirit of healing; protective male figure (English name: Longhair Kachina).

Angwusnasomtaka/Tümas: spirit of initiation of children (English name: Crow Mother).

Eototo: spirit of nature, bringer of clouds (English name: Cloud Dancer).

Kokopelli: fertility spirit, oversees childbirth and fertility. A trickster, he is also in charge of music, and is frequently depicted as a humpbacked flute player.

Nataska/Nata'aska: spirit guardian of Soyok Wuhti (Monster Woman); enforcer of good behavior in children (English name: Uncle Ogre).

Patung: spirit of healing and planting corn; can shape-shift into a badger (English name: Squash).

Toho: spirit of the hunt (English name: Mountain Lion Kachina).

⊰ YÉ'II ⊱

This is a general term for spirit beings in Navaho mythology. The Diyin Dine é (the Holy People) are considered the highest order of the Yé'ii, but there are a number of others.

THE RULERS OF THE FOUR SEAS:

TÉÉHOOLTSÓDII: Big Water Creature, The One Who Grabs Things In the Water. Ruler of the Eastern Sea. Female monster.

TÁLTL'ÁÁH ÁLÉÉH: Ruler of the Sea to the South.

CH'AL: Frog. Ruler of the Sea to the West.

II'NI' JILGAII: Winter Thunder. Ruler of the Great North Ocean.

NÍLCH'I DINE'É: the Air-Spirit People (also The Bat People).

NÍLCH'I LIGAI: the White Wind.

NÍLCH'I HA'A'AAHDĚ'GO: the East Wind.

JÓHONAA'ÉÍ (NAVAHO): The Sun, The One Who Rules the Day.

TL'ÉHONAA'ÉÍ (NAVAHO): The Moon, The One Who Rules the Night.

ASDZÁÁ NÁDLEEHÉ (NAVAHO): Changing Woman; represents a young girl's first period, and her change from girl to woman.

NA'ASHJÉ'II ASDZÁÁ (NAVAHO): Spider Woman, who knows how to spin cloth from the fibers of plants. She taught spinning to First Man and First Woman.

NAAYÉÉ' NEIZGHÁNÍ (NAVAHO): Monster Slayer; the older of the twin sons of Changing Woman, by the sun god Jóhonaa'éí.

Na'ídígishí (Navaho): He Who Cuts Life Out of the Enemy (also known as Tóbájíshchíní, Child of the Water); the younger of the twin sons of Changing Woman, by the sun god Jóhonaa'éí.

Hazéítsoh (Navaho): the Ground Squirrel Spirit; it can resemble a little old man wearing a cap with a feather in it. The faces of all ground squirrels today bear red streaks from the blood of the slain Horned Monster.

Na'azísí (Navaho): the Gopher Spirit; the backs of every gopher today are heavily furred from the hide of the slain Horned Monster.

NATIVE AMERICAN MYTHICAL MONSTERS

As in the previous section, monsters of the Inuit often have ocean connections, too.

⊰ Bináá' yee Agháni ⊱
Navaho

This is the Monster Who Kills with His Eyes; his spy is Magpie.

⊰ Déélgééd ⊱
Navaho

This is the Horned Monster.

⊰ Dichin Hastiin ⊱
Navaho

Hunger Man, the largest of twelve ravenous creatures, causes the painful suffering of hunger in people.

⚞ Hak'az Asdzáá ⚟
Navaho

This is the Cold Woman who causes the freeze that kills the crops in winter.

⚞ Kanontsistonties ⚟
Iroquois

Kanontsistonties have grotesque winged heads that fly around searching for things to eat. Because the creatures have no bodies, they can never be satiated and they are doomed to hunt forever. These creatures are frequently created as the result of a terrible act (such as murder—or even cannibalism!)

⚞ Katshituashku/Yawkwawiak ⚟
Penobscot and other tribes

Katshituashku is a man-eating bear the size of an elephant, with legs that don't bend. It has enormous teeth that can pierce many men at once.

⚞ Mishibizhiw ⚟
Sioux

Mishibizhiw is an "underwater panther" that roams rivers and lakes, waiting to drown unwary victims. The beast is a bizarre-looking concoction of a saw-blade dorsal fin, a single curved horn, a single eye, and a spiked tail that could crush a man. It may also be covered with red hair. This description sounds rather like that of an Ice Age wooly rhinoceros—or some say the skeleton of a Stegosaurus. Sioux tribal lands originally encompassed parts of the Dakotas and Montana, which are some of the richest sources of dinosaur fossils in the world.

⊰ Owl-Monster Women ⊱
Yakama

These monsters eat the world's vermin (snakes, rats, lizards, etc.), but unfortunately enjoy the tasty flesh of human children the most. The monsters are considered extremely dangerous, as the owl is a harbinger of death. Tales of other owl-like creatures abound, including the Apache "Big Owl" man-eating ogre, and the southwestern La Luchuza, which is often seen before some unfortunate luck befalls the one who saw it.

⊰ Sá ⊱
Navaho

This is the Old Age Woman, who drains the strength with the passing of years.

⊰ Sharp Elbows/ The Two-faced Monster ⊱
Sioux, and other Plains tribes

A human-like creature with literally two different faces, Sharp Elbows mutilates and/or kills its victims using its razor-like elbows. To gaze upon the Two-Faced Monster's second face is to meet death. In some traditions, one face is attractive, the other hideous.

⚔ SKINWALKERS ⚔
NAVAHO

Shamans who use their magical powers for evil, Skinwalkers can shape-shift into the form of any animal, but frequently choose revered animals such as coyotes, owls, ravens, foxes, or wolves. The purpose is to inflict pain or death on the victim.

⚔ STIKINI ⚔
CREEK AND SEMINOLE

So-called "man-owl," Stikini are evil shape-shifting witches that can assume any form, but especially like to appear as giant, undead man-eating owls by night and humans by day. Each night they are said to vomit up their entrails and hang them in trees, allowing them to shape-shift to then return at daybreak and swallow the organs to become human again. The creatures feed on human hearts, which they pull still-beating from the throats of their victims. They return to their homes with the hearts and cook them in magical pots before consuming them. A minimum of one heart a night must be consumed to keep the creatures alive.

⚔ UKTENA ⚔
CHEROKEE AND
OTHER TRIBES

One of many different monstrous snakes, Uktena is said to have terrible curved horns on its head, and to be the most difficult to kill; it bears magical scales on a body the size of a tree trunk. A scale from the creature will give a hunter good luck for the rest of his life. One of the few ways to kill it is to shoot an arrow into the seventh scale from its head.

AFRICAN AMERICANS

Not all African Americans identify with being of African descent; particularly
with regards to Caribbean countries, some African Americans identify as Haitian,
Jamaican, or Dominican, for example. The arrival of European imperialists resulted—
as it did in other parts of the New World—in the massive die-off of indigenous island
populations due to exposure to unfamiliar Old World diseases like smallpox, measles,
typhoid, and cholera. This depopulation effectively cleared the way for African slave
labor in the Caribbean and the establishment of African American populations
there. West Africans worked in the vast and lucrative sugar plantations, with the area
producing almost 90 percent of the world's consumed sugar during the seventeenth,
eighteenth, and nineteenth centuries. When slavery was outlawed, former slaves were
pushed aside and indentured "servants" were brought in from China, India, and
Southeast Asia to work the fields.

The sugar cane crop was devastating to the ecology of the islands, resulting
in depleted soils, naked hillsides, and polluted water. The production on the big
plantations declined fairly sharply in the nineteenth century, and imperial powers
such as England, France, Spain, and the US all but abandoned the Caribbean,
except for some small holdings each nation held as possessions—which became
little more than holiday playgrounds for the wealthy. The remaining West Africans
became the "native" populations of the islands. Many of these peoples migrated to
the US eventually and brought with them their legends and folktales from not only
West Africa, but also the cultures that developed in the islands. The best known of
these is Voodoo.

Voodoo (alternative spellings) is a religion with its roots in the religious
practices and beliefs of West Africa. Enslaved West Africans brought this religion
with them to the Caribbean islands and nurtured it as a means of rebellion against
their enslavers. There are many different branches of voodoo (Cuban Vodú,
Dominican Vudú, Puerto Rican Vudú, etc.), but the discussion in this section
will mainly refer to Haitian vodou and Louisiana voodoo.

The groups of slaves that brought the roots of vodou to the islands
(particularly the island of Saint-Domingue, which eventually became the nations
of Haiti and the Dominican Republic) were mainly taken from an African
kingdom that existed in the seventeenth century in what is now Nigeria, Togo,
and Benin. The word *vodu* is from the Fon dialect in the region and means
"spirit" or "god." As slaves from other parts of West Africa mingled with the

vodou practitioners, as well as the remains of indigenous Native American populations, a unique religion all their own arose. When Catholicism was imposed on the slaves by frightened white plantation owners, the rituals of that religion were added to the emerging slave belief system, and the original vodou religion of West Africa was reborn as voodoo. The term for religions that arise from a blending of several religions into one practice is a syncretic religion. Modern upper-class Haitians no longer practice voodoo, but rather Catholicism—though many in the poorer classes still follow voodoo traditions.

New Orleans was founded in 1718 and became the capital of the French-owned Louisiana Territory. The city was established by the French Mississippi Company to act as a port for staging supplies to the Caribbean and shipping refined sugar back to Europe. It was also a slave camp where the bitterest and angriest slaves were taken to be "tamed" for sale to plantation owners. The city was part of the US purchase of the Louisiana Territory in 1803, and that change of ownership coincided with a series of slave uprisings in Haiti—which were fueled by the spiritual beliefs of the voodoo religion. The revolts eventually drove the French from the island, and most of them fled to New Orleans—taking many of their French-speaking, voodoo-practicing slaves with them. So, voodoo became established in New Orleans and spread to other places in the US Southern states; it changed and grew as it spread, becoming a well-established if highly variable living system of beliefs.

Unlike the religions of many indigenous populations, voodoo is monotheistic. This theology is the heart of Catholicism, which we know had a huge influence on voodoo. In practice, voodoo believers, called Vodouisants, superimposed the Catholic saints over the top of their own native gods/spirits to get around the strict limitations placed on the practicing of their African religions.

Voodoo is not the only religion imported from the Caribbean, of course. Santeria Lucumi (from Cuba), Espiritismo (Puerto Rico), Kumina (Jamaica), and Quimbois (Martinique)—as well as practices from parts of Latin and South America—also gained followers in the US.

It is important to understand when looking at the religious influences on African Americans that we must include the major religions—particularly Christianity and Islam, and to a lesser extent Judaism. While Catholicism was pressed on many early New World African Americans, huge numbers of them willingly embraced various Christian religions, especially Methodist and Baptist sects. Roughly 80 percent of African Americans currently identify as Christians, with somewhere between 2 percent and 8 percent self-identifying as Muslims. So, while we speak of syncretic religions in this discussion, recognize that these religions apply to a relatively small number of African Americans.

VOODOO AND SANTERIA GODS AND GODDESSES

There are few actual "gods" in voodoo-type religions, partly due to the influence of Catholic suppression. There are, however, many "spirits" with god-like capabilities. Some are presented here.

⚜ BONDYE ⚜
HAITI

Bondye is the "good god," the supreme being of the voodoo religion. Bondye is the creator and the highest principle in the universe (much like the Brahman in Hindu religion). Bondye is the eternal everything, embodiment of the human experience and the bringer of order from the chaos. He created all life, and all life therefore belongs to him. Things are considered "good" if they strengthen the bonds of humanity, and "bad" if they disrupt those bonds. The name Bondye is derived from the Creole French *bon dieu*, meaning "good god."

⊰ Lwa/Loa ⊱
Haiti

Lwa are the spirit intermediaries between humans and the supreme god Bondye. Because Bondye himself is too complex for human understanding or interaction, the Lwa are consulted when humanity needs help, and they may either act directly with those who summon them, or may intercede with Bondye on behalf of the summoner. In this manner, they are much like the Catholic saints (whose positions were "assimilated" into the voodoo religion). The Lwa can be subdivided into three categories (called "families") below.

RADA are spirits of West African/Old World origin, generally considered benevolent creator-types; their color association is white.

PETRO/PETWO are spirits whose origin is Haitian; they are New World spirits, typically considered more "aggressive" than Rada, and concerned with deeper—perhaps "darker"—topics such as life and death, revenge, and anger. Their color association is red.

GHEDE/GUÉDÉ are spirits associated with the dead, they act to transport souls, celebrate irreverence, and encourage sexuality and the sex act. They serve as reminders of the goodness of life despite death. Their color association is black. The chief of the Ghede is Baron Samedi (spelling varies), made famous by the James Bond movie, *Live and Let Die*.

None of the Lwa should be judged as being "good" or "evil," they are neither. They are more like chaotic neutral, acting as they see fit without the bounds of human morality or social concerns.

⊰ Orishas ⊱
Cuba

Spirits of the Santeria Lucumi religion, orishas fill the same function as the Lwa of voodoo. The religion of Santeria Lucumi is similar to that of voodoo, with original African beliefs (this time from Yoruba-speaking people rather than Fon-speaking people) of enslaved peoples who were brought to Cuba rather than to

Saint-Domingue. Again, the Catholic saints and rituals were superimposed on the Yoruban spirits in order to get around restrictions on native religions. Lucumi orishas are associated with Catholic saints; only a few of the hundreds of original African orishas have a presence in Santeria.

AGANYU: Orisha governing the violence of natural earth processes such as earthquakes and volcanic eruptions. This spirit appropriately has a hot temper, and he can also be appealed to for relief from fevers. His color association is red, and his Catholic saint is Saint Christopher, lending Aganyu dominion over travelers as well.

BABALU-AYE: Orisha of sickness and healing, patron orisha of beggars, the sick, and the disabled. He can cause infections as easily as he can heal them, and his Catholic equivalent is Saint Lazarus, the leper who was raised from the dead and healed by Christ. The colors of Babalu-Aye are purple and light blue.

CHANGO/SHANGO: Orisha of thunder, lightning, and fire; he can be invoked to exact revenge or bring justice to the wronged. Chango is a violent and powerful orisha, given to rages and outlandish behavior, as well as causing death by electrocution or fire. Not surprisingly, Chango is also a symbol of male strength and virility and is a notorious womanizer. This orisha is variously associated with Saints Barbara, Mark, Jerome, Elijah, Expeditus, or Bartholomew. His colors are red and white.

ELLEGUA/ESHU: Ellegua is the most powerful orisha other than Obatala. He is the orisha of secrets and mysteries, opening doorways, and facilitating new experiences. He is also appealed to by travelers. He is a messenger to the other orishas, a warrior, and a trickster; he is a ruler of crossroads and can see the past, present, and future. He tends to be mischievous, childlike, and teasing (he adores children)—but can also be clever, sly, and devilish. He is known to cause accidents and injuries involving bleeding. He is sometimes associated with Satan for his trickster ways, but Ellegua is *not* evil. His colors are red and black.

OBATALA: The creator of all living things and the earth itself and the father of many of the orishas, he is the oldest of them and looks after the others. He is the Sky Father, the King of Kings, and the patron orisha of leadership, knowledge, justice, the handicapped and the military. He is a former warrior who atones for the atrocities he witnessed in war via his own compassion and patience. His wife is Yamana, the orisha of the oceans. Obatala is the only orisha who embodies both male and female qualities. His color is pure white.

OSAIN: Orisha of nature, forests, and herbal healing; Osain is the patron of hunters and the home. Osain presents with a single leg, single arm, single ear, and single eye. He uses a crutch made from a twisted tree branch, and is usually associated with Pope Saint Sylvester I (though associations with Saints John, Joseph, and others also occur). Osain's colors are red, green, white, and yellow.

OSHUN: Orisha of love, fertility, and marriage; Oshun is one of the few female orishas and is in charge of the lower abdomen and genitalia. She has far-ranging associations with feminine beauty, human relationships, fresh water, and relief from drought. She is commonly associated with the Virgin Mary, particularly in Oshun aspect as Our Lady of Charity, who provides hope and helps ensure survival on the seas. Our Lady of Charity is the patron saint of Cuba, the home of Santeria. Oshun's colors are red, green, amber, violet, yellow, and coral—in celebration of her transformation into a peacock in myth.

AMERICAN MYTHICAL MONSTERS

The monsters represented here are from a variety of sources, which may themselves be "mythical." None of this is dogma; mythology and folklore are passed mainly through oral traditions, and as such are subject to a tremendous amount of variation in the telling. Additionally, since the very nature of syncretic religions is to be an amalgam of other traditions, inconsistencies are common. Here is a list of some of the monsters of American myth.

⊰ BEAST OF BLADENBORO ⊱
NORTH CAROLINA, US

In the mid-1950s, a creature described as "a large cat" made off with a number of dogs in the area. Reports rolled in regarding missing livestock as well, and hysteria peaked when the bodies of dead dogs were allegedly found drained of blood. Hunters from around the country descended on Bladenboro with the expectation of bagging the beast. Eventually, someone shot a bobcat and the poor animal was displayed as "the beast" so that the overzealous hunters would leave. Bladenboro continues to celebrate the mythical monster with a beast-fest each year in October.

⊰ Bigfoot/Sasquatch ⊱
Pacific Northwest US

Everybody knows about this monster: 7–9 feet (2–3 meters) tall, hairy all over, long swinging arms and *huge* feet. It manages to stay hidden in the well-trampled Pacific North woods, stubbornly resisting having its picture taken. While capable of causing terrific harm due to its enormous size and strength, Bigfoot is rarely reported as having actually hurt anyone (or anything, unless you count the game it kills to feed itself). Almost 30 percent of polled Americans admit to believing in Bigfoot, with nearly the same number of Canadian believers. Several TV shows have devoted their programming to the

lore and (hopefully) capture of live Bigfeet. Most of these shows have subsequently been canceled, without ever having accomplished their goal. Bigfoot is a cash cow in the area, so his continuing to be "at large" (pun intended) is beneficial to the inhabitants of his homeland. Some say that the Wendigo (another large beast/spirit, this time of Native American myth) is the same creature. However, the Wendigo's association with cannibalism (and its description as topping 15 feet [4.5 meters] in height) would indicate otherwise.

⊰ Chupacabra ⊱
Mexico and Southwest US

The name of this creature, Chupacabra, of Mexican–American myth is translated as "goat sucker," and it is said to drain the blood of livestock. It looks like some sort of mangy bear or dog, though supposed "specimens" of the beasts, when photographed, are nearly always dead. The creatures are also seen in Puerto Rico and other Latin countries.

⚏ GOWROW ⚏
BAYOU SOUTH

Another monster of the South, this one is a lake inhabitant that gets its name from the hideous sound it makes. In turn of the twentieth-century Arkansas, the creature was described as being 20 feet (6 meters) long and reptilian, with enormous tusks that could kill large livestock.

⚏ HODAG ⚏
WISCONSIN, US

One of the strangest American monsters, the Hodag is native to the woods of Wisconsin, and it is ferocious. There are several subspecies of Hodag, and the beast has become the official mascot of the city of Rhinelander, WI. It is stated to have horns, an elephant-like grin (elephants grin?), the spiked back of a dinosaur, and various other undesirable traits. A famously-faked photo from the very early turn of the twentieth century (a time famously famous for fabulous fakes), shows townsmen surrounding a (purportedly dead) Hodag with their spears and axes at the ready. An unfortunate boy lies unconscious (dead?) in the foreground. A well-known huckster claimed to have captured one alive, only admitting it was a hoax when representatives of the Smithsonian Institution threatened to come investigate it.

⚏ JACKALOPE ⚏
TEXAS

So bizarre it's comical, this creature (shown only in pictures and taxidermy specimens) consists of a large jackrabbit which sports the antlers of an antelope or deer. The animals mate during electrical storms, yet are somehow extinct—despite continuing to appear in souvenir shops across the West. Theorists believe that the legend began with the sightings of rabbits which were infected with the (very real) Shope papilloma virus, which causes infected animals to sprout horny growths on their faces and heads.

⚜ JERSEY DEVIL ⚜
NEW JERSEY, US

Back when New Jersey actually had much more wilderness (the 1700s), the deeply religious settlers of the area told of a demon born to a human woman, which would fly through the woods emitting wailing, high-pitched cries. It has the head of a horse, with the wings and claws of a demon.

⚜ LA LLORONA ⚜
SOUTHWEST

The "weeping woman" of a New Mexico myth, La Llorona is the ghost of a woman who drowned her sons in a jealous rage, then went insane with her own guilt. She either starved to death on the banks of the river where she drowned them, or she alternatively threw herself into the same river and also drowned. Her ghost returns to haunt the riverbanks and kill other young children who venture too close to the water. She can be seen wearing a white gown, walking up and down the riverside as she screams and wails in grief.

⚜ LOVELAND FROG ⚜
OHIO, US

While earlier reports were dismissed, this creature became famous when two different police officers from the same jurisdiction reported sighting it on separate occasions two weeks apart. It was described as about 3 feet (1 meter) tall, with webbed hands and feet, and a face like a frog. Neither officer would describe the creature as a "monster," but rather insisted that they thought it was a lost household pet!

⚔ Lugaroo, also Rougarou ⚔
Louisiana

A corruption of the Cajun French *loup garou* (spellings vary), this creature is essentially a werewolf. Lugaroo are shape-shifters who transform from human to wolf-like animals *at will* (without being dependent on the moon phase), and suck the blood of their victims. They also keep their human minds while in their wolf form. Derived from Haitian myth, the creatures are said to exchange the blood of their victims for magical powers via a pact with Satan or some other demon. It's known by many other names: Soucouyant/

Soucriant (Dominica, Saint Lucia, Guadeloupe), Ole-Higue/Ole Haig (Guyana, Jamaica), Asema (Suriname), and Hag (Bahamas).

⚔ Mothman ⚔
West Virginia, US

First spotted in the 1960s, this creature was said to be 7 feet (2 meters) tall with the wings of a bat—or sometimes fluttery like a butterfly. Since it flies at night, it was dubbed "Mothman" by the press. Sightings were regular, if not particularly common, until a tragic accident involving the collapse of a major automobile bridge resulted in dozens of deaths. Mothman sightings ceased afterward, leaving some to wonder if the creature was trying to warn—or waiting to act.

⊰ SKUNK APE ⊱
FLORIDA AND GEORGIA

In the American South (especially Florida), this creature is notorious for its smell—which is extreme. It is an urban myth that makes the rounds from time to time, most recently in 2000 in Florida. It is blamed for death and injury to animals, especially livestock. Some say the animal is a Bigfoot relative, but distinguished from its much bigger cousin by having only four toes to Bigfoot's five. There's a Skunk Ape gift shop in Everglades National Park.

⊰ SLENDERMAN ⊱

This is the newest monster phenomenon—a being created by a person on the internet. Started in 2009 by a Florida man on a monster website, Slenderman soon went viral and thousands of fans embellished his legend, giving him a life of his own. The monster was so successful, it actually drove two Wisconsin teens to stab their classmate nineteen times in an effort to "please" the creature, which they claim they believed was real. The crime was glamourized in a Hollywood movie.

⊰ WAMPUS [CAT] ⊱
MID-SOUTH, US

Half woman, half wildcat, this monster has yellow fangs, glowing eyes, and reeks like a sewer. It is said to kill animals and kidnap (presumably to eat?) young children. Stories tell of a Cherokee wife who hid beneath a mountain lion skin to spy on her husband, and was punished by being doomed to wear the skin of the mountain lion for eternity.

AMERICAN SUPERSTITIONS

A great number of American superstitions are a result of our multicultural heritage. Here are some of them.

KNOCK ON WOOD is said to avert bad luck that results from either talking about a subject that is taboo, or from accidentally committing an unlucky act (such as spilling the salt shaker). The belief arises from pagan mythology that benevolent spirits live in trees, and that touching the tree lets you tap the kindness of the spirit inside.

"SEE A PENNY, PICK IT UP, and all the day you'll have good luck!" This quirky superstition is amusing because the rhyme is supposed to be chanted along with the act of picking up the penny. Essentially, this amounts to an invocation spoken to drive away demons that might be thinking about doing you harm. This works with any coin, not just pennies. Be aware, though, that the coin must be face up; face down negates the luck.

BAD NEWS (OR DEATH) COMES IN THREES is a curious superstition which seems to be most relevant when referring to the deaths of celebrities or other people of note, rather than the general public. "Threes" are generally considered cosmically "balanced" (consider the Christian Trinity, or the Hindu Trimurti), so this superstition may be connected to the Fates, mystical demi-goddesses of Greek mythology who determine the lifespan of mortals. There are three Fates: Clotho ("The Spinner" of the thread of life), Lachesis ("The Allotter," who determines the length of the thread), and Atropos ("The Inflexible," who cuts the thread of life).

BEGINNER'S LUCK is meant to be humbling, with its implication that the "successful player" in either games of chance or risks in life owes their achievement to some mystical force, which cannot be counted on to help his or her succeed again. In other words, don't take risks. Play it safe, because next time you will fail. This is a very anti-individual/pro-community stance.

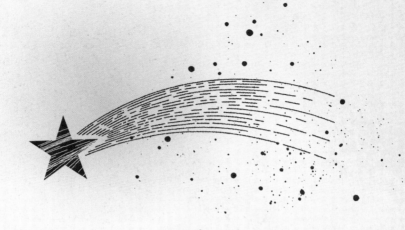

WISH ON A FALLING STAR is almost magical—the belief that the death of a celestial body is somehow fortuitous for the earthbound is almost sinful; it likely would have been frowned upon as "pagan" by the Church.

CROSS YOUR FINGERS FOR LUCK comes from the belief in the power of the Holy Cross, so "crossing your fingers" connotes a *blessing* of sorts on the forthcoming endeavor (even if that endeavor is just an attempted field goal after a touchdown). Curiously, many children (and no small number of adults) also believe that "crossing your fingers"—especially when hidden from view—somehow negates any promises you make while those fingers are crossed. It is a way of excusing your intention to lie despite your promise to behave! Parents, however, do not share equal belief in the crossed fingers excuse.

LUCKY FOUR-LEAF CLOVERS is an Irish superstition which stems from their belief that a shamrock (with its three leaves) represents the Holy Trinity (a belief that arose after the introduction of Christianity to Ireland). The shamrock leaves stand for faith (God), love (Jesus), and hope (the Holy Spirit); the fourth leaf, however, stands for luck, and the rarity of the fourth leaf gives the tradition magical status.

NUMBER 13 is bad, 7 is good, 666 is deadly! But why? Well, there were 12 apostles at the Last Supper—unless you count Judas, who betrayed Christ. Judas' betrayal and his status as the thirteenth apostle has forever cast the number 13 into the fiery pit of terrible numbers—if you're Christian. Along the same lines, 666 is Biblical; it is the "number of the beast," heralding the arrival of the anti-Christ in Revelation at the end of the New Testament:

> *"Here is a call for wisdom: Let the one who has insight*
> *calculate the number of the beast, for it is the number of a man,*
> *and that number is 666."*
> [Revelation 13:18]

Notice that the chapter from the Book of Revelation that contains this verse is number 13!

———————

7 IS LUCKY for many reasons: classical astronomy noted seven celestial bodies that were visible to the unaided eye: the sun, the moon, Mercury, Venus, Mars, Jupiter, and Saturn. A number of religions named seven primary gods to rule these planets (the Greeks and Romans, the Egyptians, and the Japanese); the Arabs built seven holy temples; the Hindus describe seven chakras; Buddhism describes seven incarnations of the Buddha. The Old Testament is chock-full of sevens: the world was created in six days, plus one day of rest; King Solomon's temple took seven years to build; the Hebrew Torah describes every seventh year of the Jewish calendar as a holy year; the Kabbalah uses a red string bracelet with seven knots to ward against the evil eye; seven seals must be broken in Revelation to bring about Armageddon; there are seven deadly sins, seven plagues on Egypt, seven heavenly virtues, and seven sacraments; shiva is sat for seven days. There are seven hills of Rome, and seven seas; there are seven continents, seven wonders of the world, seven colors in the visible spectrum (think *rainbow*), and seven musical notes on a scale. And don't forget the Seven Dwarfs! Mystically speaking, the seventh son of a seventh son will be a seer, while the seventh daughter of a seventh daughter will be a witch.

Mexico and Central America

Mexico's history is long and storied, marked by centuries of indigenous occupation and conquest. First inhabited over thirteen thousand years ago, it was the same wave of migration over the Bering land bridge after the last Ice Age that brought what would become Mexico's "indigenous" population into the region—with many of those people continuing to move south down through Central and South America. A number of advanced civilizations thrived in Mexico and Central America, beginning with the Olmecs. The Olmecs flourished from about 1500 to about 400 BCE, establishing the framework for the other civilizations that would follow them. Olmec religion was based on the actions of priests and shamans, and it was dependent on the ruling elite to act as the bridge between the gods and the people. The Olmecs left no written record of their mythology, though it has been discovered that the familiar "Feathered Serpent" and a rain deity were part of the pantheon. The Olmec name for the Feathered Serpent god is unknown.

The Mayans

The next great civilization following the Olmecs was the Maya, with the first of the great Mayan cities rising around 750 BCE, and continuing until a major collapse of the system around 900 CE. The collapse did not result in the elimination of the Maya people, but saw instead a shift in the population away from the urban centers such as Tikal in the low-lying jungle areas around Guatemala and Belize, to the drier Yucatán Peninsula of southeastern Mexico.

In the Yucatán, the great city of Chichén Itzá was built, and it was dedicated to the Feathered Serpent, now named Kukulkan. This god had his roots in the earlier, pre-collapse Mayan society and was known then as Waxaklahun Ubah Kan, the War Serpent. Again, much of his mythology is unknown. The complex at Chichén Itzá, while amazing, was significantly less grand than those built prior to the Mayan collapse, marked by fewer monumental architectural constructions.

One known precept of Mayan mythology was the idea of a "divine king." Much like the pharaohs of Egypt, the Mayan king was believed to be descended directly from the gods. This is why the royal bloodline was so important; the blood of gods must remain unsullied from intermingling with the common people, lest the god-king lose his powers and fail to perform the rituals required to keep Mayan civilization running smoothly. Royalty passed from father to eldest son, and with it the power of the gods. Major cities such as Chichén Itzá had temple-pyramids topped by altars, where

the rituals of bloodletting and human sacrifice took place. The Mesoamerican pantheon (including that of the Maya) evolved from the earliest primitive religions of elemental worship (fire, water, earth, nature); the addition of astral bodies (the sun, moon, planets, and stars) broadened the ideology, as did the introduction of zoomorphic deities.

MAYAN GODS AND GODDESSES

There are an estimated two hundred or so Mayan gods and goddesses. The following section takes a look at just a few of them.

⇥ CHAAC ⇤

The mighty rain god of the Maya, Chaac is so powerful that he has four aspects, which correspond to the four cardinal directions and their colors: North = white, South = yellow, East = red, West = black. This great god with his bulging eyes brings thunder, lightning, clouds, and most importantly life-giving rain. Chaac may be a later addition to the pantheon, as the Maya previously lived in tropical jungles and would not have been as dependent upon a rain god as they would come to be in the arid Yucatán peninsula.

⊰ THE HEROIC TWINS ⊱

The Heroic Twins are an archetype found across many civilizations of the world, including the Romans (Romulus and Remus), the Navaho (Naayéé' Neizghání and Na'ídígishí), and the Greek (Castor and Pollux). The Heroic Twins in Mayan mythology are named Hunahpú and Xbalanqué. In the Popol Vuh (the post-colonial record of Mayan mythology), the stories of the Heroic Twins tell of two boys who, among many brave deeds, descended into the underworld (Xibalba—perhaps this became Cibola, the fabled city of gold?) to confront the lords there who had tricked the original and first set of Heroic Twins into playing the sacred ball game with them—and then brutally killing them. The original twins were named One Hunahpú and Seven Hunahpú. A long story describes how Hunahpú and Xbalanqué avenged the deaths of their father (One Hunahpú) and uncle. The boys were divine and were able to entreat the wild animals to help them trick, and eventually defeat, the Lords of Xibalba and bring about their deaths.

⊰ HUNAB KU ⊱

Hunab Ku is a pre-Columbian Mesoamerican god whose name translates as "The One God" or "The Sole God." Believed by scholars to predate the Spanish conquest, Hunab Ku was exploited by Spanish priests as a means of convincing the Maya to convert to Catholicism.

⊰ ITZAM CAB AIN ⊱

The Great Earth Crocodile, Itzam Cab Ain's death made the earth (also known as the Peten) following the Great Flood that destroyed the failed mud people and wood people the creators had made.

⊰ ITZAMNA ⊱

One of the original Maya creator gods, Itzamna taught writing and medicine to the people. He is the father of the Bacabs, who set the sacred trees at the four corners of the earth. Itzamna is sometimes known as Hunab Ku, or as Kinich Ahau the Sun God.

⚜ Ix Chel ⚜

Goddess of midwifery and childbirth, as well as medicine, she is depicted as a crone.

⚜ Kinich Ahau ⚜

The Mayan Sun god, Kinich Ahau is sometimes considered to be an aspect of—or to be associated with—the creator god Itzamna. During the high period of Mayan civilization, "Kinich Ahau" was used as a royal title, connoting the divinity of kings. In some codices, this god may be referred to as God G. He appears in many temple carvings.

⚜ Tonsured Maize God ⚜

One of several maize gods, the Tonsured Maize god is the personification of maize, cacao beans, and jade. He presides over the scribing arts, dance, and feasting. On holy days, Mayan kings would dress up as the Tonsured Maize god, who is easily distinguished in Mayan hieroglyphic writings by his unusual hairstyle.

MAYAN MYTHICAL MONSTERS (AND DEMONS)

Much of Mayan mythology derives from the religions of the indigenous peoples of the area. They contain elements of Mexican and South American tribal beliefs. As in many polytheistic religions, there is a mixture of spirits, demons, and true monsters.

⚜ Aluxes ⚜

Not exactly monsters, Aluxes are believed to be the spirits of Maya ancestors (or sometimes creatures like nymphs and dryads) that inhabit the lands and jungles of the Maya. The creatures appear to be miniature versions of Maya, and they may behave mischievously if they feel that they have been disrespected. Farmers are expected to ask permission of the Aluxes before plowing a field, and builders must ask the Aluxes for their blessings before building bridges or other structures on their lands.

⚜ CAMAZOTZ/CAMOAZOTZ ⚜

Camazotz is the vampire bat god of death, the night, and sacrifice. It rules the night, living in caves and grottos away from human habitations. It was Camazotz who took the head of the heroic twin Hunahpú and used it as a soccer ball. He is frequently depicted as holding a knife in one hand and his victim in the other.

⚜ ONE DEATH AND SEVEN DEATH ⚜

As the Lords of Xibalba, the Mayan underworld, it is they who invite the original heroic twins One Hunahpú and Seven Hunahpú down to Xibalba to play the sacred ballgame. After the twins accept, they are put through a number of challenges before being allowed to play the game. When the brothers fail in the challenges, the lords murder and dismember them, placing One Hunahpú's head in a tree.

THE AZTECS

The most recent indigenous group to influence Mexican mythology were the Aztecs. This wandering warrior tribe (who referred to themselves as *Mexíca* or *Meshica*) originally came from northern Mexico, and they took control of central Mexico through force of combat. In an agreement to stop the constant civil war among the tribes, two other city-states agreed to form a triumvirate with the Aztec capital of Tenochtitlán. Located on an island in the middle of Lake Texcoco—the area now at the center of Mexico City—Tenochtitlán soon held all the power, due to its superior military might.

As previously mentioned, the Feathered Serpent (Quetzalcoatl to the Aztecs) was long a god among the peoples of Mexico and Central America. It was the Toltec civilization that changed the name of the god from Kukulkan to Quetzalcoatl. The Aztecs were a nomadic tribe that wandered the southwest US and northern Mexico, looking for a sign. The "sign" was the image of a snake doing battle with an eagle. When they saw this image, they would know that they had found their homeland. The chimera of a bird-serpent must have seemed tailor made for them, and they took their "homeland" from the Toltecs they conquered, and set down roots.

AZTEC GODS AND GODDESSES

Aztec mythology shares much with other Mexican tribal mythologies, as is common in the region. As one civilization rose on the remains of the previous, the tribes absorbed and adapted pieces of mythologies into their own.

⊰ HUITZILOPOCHTLI ⊱
HUMMINGBIRD

Huitzilopochtli is the god of war, the supreme god in the Aztec pantheon. Note that much of what is known about Aztec mythology is taken from sources that were deliberately rewritten in the early 1400s by order of an Aztec emperor determined to legitimize the supremacy of his god, as well as his own royal descent from that god. The Hummingbird God's color is blue.

⊰ QUETZALCOATL ⊱

Quetzalcoatl is the Feathered (or "Plumed") Serpent, or god of the air. His color is white. The Feathered Serpent is the one god who was passed from the Olmecs to the Maya to the Aztecs with very little change.

⚄ TECUCIZTECATL ⚄
THE ONE FROM THE PLACE OF THE CONCH

Tecuciztecatl is a wealthy god from an unnamed sea ("the place of the conch") who vies with Nanahuatzin for the right to be the fifth sun. His failure leads him to become the moon.

⚄ TEZCATLIPOCA ⚄
SMOKING MIRROR

Aztec god of the earth and soil, as well as night, enmity, and discord, this god is a trickster who often disguises himself in order to prank or even harm the poor unfortunate victim. He is credited with humiliating and dethroning the last great Toltec king (Huemac), bringing about the downfall of the Toltec civilization. Tezcatlipoca was the most powerful of the four children of the Dual God, Ometeotl. His color is black.

⚄ XOCHIQUETZAL ⚄
FLOWER QUETZAL FEATHER

Xochiquetzal is the goddess of beauty and young women. From her hair, a woman would be made for one of the sons of a man.

AZTEC MYTHICAL MONSTERS

Aztec monsters reflect many of the same characteristics as those of Native American tribes.

⚔ Ahuizotl ⚔

Ahuizotl is a dog-like creature with waterproof hair that lives in or near water, and has a love of eating human flesh; it is said to be especially fond of teeth, nails, and eyes. It has two hands instead of paws, plus an additional hand on the end of its tail, that it uses to grab unwary victims and pull them underwater, drowning them.

⚔ Cihuateteo ⚔
Divine Women

These are malevolent spirits of women who died in childbirth. On earth, they become demons who haunt crossroads, where they steal children, and tempt men to madness and adultery. Shrines are still erected at crossroads to appease them.

⚔ Nagual/Nahual ⚔

These are human shape-shifters who can turn themselves into various animals. Often a shaman or priest, the would-be shape-shifter is believed to have made a pact with the devil to gain their magical abilities.

⚔ Tlaltecuhtli "Earth Lord" ⚔

Tlaltecuhtli is a giant female sea monster. She is covered with mouths all over her body and a ravenous eater of flesh. Quetzalcoatl and Tezcatlipoca turned themselves into even bigger sea monsters and tore Tlaltecuhtli in two, making her top half the new earth (after the flood) and her bottom half the new heavens. Her screams of pain caused the other gods to transform her: Her hair became trees, shrubs, and flowers, and grasses grew from her skin. Fresh water poured from her eyes to make the rivers, wells, and streams. her many mouths became the caves of the world. Mountains and valleys were made from her nose. Though no longer a monster, Tlaltecuhtli still needed fresh blood and flesh. So, once the people were created, they made sacrifices to feed her. Thus, the earth continues to provide all the things that people and animals need to live.

⊰ QUINAMETZIN ⊱

These are the race of giants created by Quetzalcoatl to populate the earth during the age of the first sun. They are described as being over 10 feet (3 meters) tall and weighing about a quarter of a ton. The great cities of Tenochtitlán and Tehuacán—among others—were allegedly built by these giants.

Contemporary Mexican Myths and Legends

When we look at contemporary Mexican myth and legend, we see much of their ancestral Native American forebears, as well as the huge influence of Catholicism, which arrived with the Spanish conquistadors. Over 80 percent of Mexican adults identify themselves as Catholic (over 96 million people), compared with only 20 percent of US citizens identifying as such. As the Mexican people are descended from indigenous, Spanish, and mixed-race (*mestizo*) peoples, so too are their legends and folklore a representation of a mixture of origins. An example are the Chacs—ancient rain spirits which are said to be controlled by Jesus Christ. Arguably, it is the Virgin of Guadalupe who is the most recognized and revered Mexican religious figure. Since her miraculous appearance to a peasant named Juan Diego in 1531, the Virgin is worshiped as a divine being and credited with stopping the spread of epidemics, as well as with inspiring movements towards liberation and independence.

A number of historical figures have made their way into legend as well. Malinche, an indigenous (likely Aztec) woman who helped Hernán Cortés overcome the Aztec ruler and bring about the fall of the Aztec empire, has been traditionally reviled as a traitor to her people. More recently, Mexican women artists and writers have tried to build a more balanced view of Malinche.

Priest and leader for Mexican independence, Father Miguel Hidalgo y Costilla is a national hero who died by firing squad. Similarly, Francisco "Pancho" Villa, a bandit who became a Revolutionary general, and Emiliano Zapata, a peasant who fought for the rights of peasants during the war for independence, have gained the status of legends for their purported deeds. In fact, Zapata, it is believed, will one day return to again save his people. If you listen in the dark, you might be able to hear the hoofbeats of his faithful horse, Lightning, as the two thunder through the villages at night.

A fascinating folktale describes a peasant who is so desperately hungry that he steals a chicken and cooks it. A stranger approaches and asks for some food, but the peasant refuses to share. The stranger then reveals himself to be God, and the peasant says that he surely won't share his food with God because God favors the rich and burdens the poor. God leaves and another stranger appears; again, the peasant refuses to share. The second stranger reveals himself to be Death, and now the peasant says he will surely share with Death because Death is fair, taking rich and poor, young and old equally.

MEXICAN AND CENTRAL AMERICAN SUPERSTITIONS

The superstitions of Mexicans and Central American peoples often center around bodily harm. These beliefs gave rise to the creation of *milagros*, or amulets believed to have magical healing and protective powers.

PUTTING A HAT on the bed brings bad luck.

CLEANSING WITH AN egg can avert the evil eye, especially against children. A raw egg is rolled over the victim's body to absorb the bad energy from the evil eye. The same egg is then cracked into a bowl of water and placed under the victim's bed overnight. If the egg curdles, the person has been cured of the evil eye.

PUTTING YOUR PURSE on the floor will cause you to become poor.

IF SOMEONE SWEEPS your feet and you're single, you'll never marry.

STANDING A BROOM upside down behind your door will cause unwanted guests to leave!

DECORATING YOUR HOUSE with sea shells is bad luck.

KEEP A FULL glass of water on top of the fridge or behind a door to absorb negative energy from the home.

DON'T IRON YOUR clothes and then go wash your hands—if you do, you'll get arthritis.

STEPPING OUTSIDE IN a sudden cold snap can make you go blind.

LIKEWISE, IF YOU go outside after eating too much, your face will become paralyzed.

EAT SOME CHOCOLATE if a scorpion stings you.

IF YOU DROP a tortilla on the floor, company is coming.

IF YOU SLEEP with a dog or a cat, you will become infertile.

DON'T HAND SOMEONE a salt shaker—it's bad luck. Set the shaker down in front of them and let them pick it up themselves.

IF YOU STARE at a dog while it poops, you'll get a pimple in your eye!

DON'T POINT AT a rainbow or you'll get a pimple on your nose.

IF YOU SEE something ugly while you're pregnant, your baby will turn out ugly too.

DON'T TAKE A bath while pregnant or the dirty water will reach your baby.

BABIES WHO DON'T listen to music while in the uterus will come out deaf.

IF YOU SMILE at a baby, be sure to touch it or you will make the baby sick.

DON'T CUT YOUR child's fingernails before their first birthday or they will have poor vision.

EAT TWELVE GRAPES at midnight on New Year's Eve—one for every stroke of twelve o'clock. Make a wish for each grape you eat.

PACK A SUITCASE and walk around the block on New Year's Eve to ensure safe travels and good luck.

THROWING A BUCKET of water out of a window on New Year's Eve will help wash away the past year and let you start clean in the new year.

TELL SOMEONE ABOUT your nightmares to keep them from coming true.

WHEN DOGS HOWL, death is near.

South America

South America lies mostly in the Southern Hemisphere; the mountains hug the west coast while the jungles of the Amazon basin occupy most of the northern half of the continent. The largest country by far is Brazil, the fifth-largest nation in the world and greater in size than the continent of Australia (with nearly ten times that country's population). Brazil is also the only country in South America that speaks Portuguese; it was claimed for Portugal in 1500 by explorer Pedro Cabral.

While the impact of the European conquest on recent South American history cannot be minimized, it is the influence of indigenous peoples—particularly the Inca—that had the greatest effect on the mythology of the continent. Evidence of human occupation of South America can be traced back some eleven thousand years and includes a variety of native tribes such as the Arawaks, the Guaranis, and the Tupis. Many of these tribes were subdivided by religious practices and social stratification, as a great number of indigenous peoples are. Tribal relations were marked by near-constant warfare over social mores, resources, and cultural institutions.

The Incas

The Incas were to South America what the Mayans were to Central America and Mexico. Flourishing from about 1400 to 1533 CE, the vast Incan Empire at its height covered the entire western half of the continent from Ecuador to Chile, making it the largest empire in the Americas and the greatest empire in the world at the time. The center of Incan civilization was located in what's now Peru, and their capital was Cusco/Cuzco/Qosqo. Currently listed as a UNESCO World Heritage site, this city was laid out in the shape of the sacred puma (mountain lion) or jaguar (also sacred to the Maya) and housed a population of approximately 150,000 people. The center of the site was the Temple of the Sun, located in the religious complex known as Coricancha/Qorikancha. The complex occupied the area that is the tail of the jaguar/puma, and it was dedicated to a number of gods in the Inca pantheon, including Viracocha, the creator god, Quilla, the moon goddess (also Mama Kilya), and most especially to Inti, the sun god. The Inca believed they were descended from Inti. Legends still say that Coricancha was a city of gold, with extensive layering of sheet gold on doors and other architectural features, along with the studding of precious gems (especially emeralds) on the buildings made for a mind-boggling sight when the Spaniards (led by Pizarro) invaded Peru. Gold was believed by the Incas to be the sweat of the sun, while silver was the tears of the moon.

INCAN GODS AND GODDESSES

The Inca religion had a large pantheon of powerful gods and goddesses, rather than spirit intermediaries. Here are some of them.

⊰ AI-APAEC ⊱
ALSO AYAPEC

The only record of this god's existence seems to be in the few pieces of pottery and sculpture that the Moche people left behind when they abandoned (or were erased from) their lands near Lake Titicaca. The effigy of Ayapec shows him holding a knife in one claw and a severed head in the other.

⊰ AXO-MAMA/AXOMAMA/ACSUMAMA ⊱

Axo-mama is the goddess of potatoes. The potato (along with the tomato) is a member of the nightshade family (which includes the poisonous belladonna plant) and is native to South America. It is an important food crop for Andean peoples.

⊰ Chasca ⊱

Chasca is the goddess of the dawn and dusk, as well as flowers; she is protector of young girls and virgins.

⊰ Cocamama ⊱
ALSO Mama Kuka

Goddess of health and happiness, this goddess demonstrates an interesting outlook on life held by the Inca: Cocamama is responsible for the production of the native coca plant—from which cocaine would eventually be derived. In Inca times, the leaves of the plant were chewed in order to gain the narcotic effect, which was believed to confer "health and happiness" upon the consumer.

⊰ Copacati ⊱

Copacati is the goddess of Lake Titicaca, the ancestral lake of the Inca. She can be vengeful, and was said to have sunk an entire town in the lake as punishment for their failure to worship her. She is frequently depicted as a serpent or snake.

⊰ Illapa ⊱

God of thunder and weather, Illapa brings the rain that waters the sacred maize crop. Illapa is usually depicted as wearing brightly shining robes or armor, and carrying both a war club and a sling.

⊰ Inti ⊱

The sun god and the god of agriculture, Inti is the most important god in the Inca pantheon. Inca emperors (Inca Sapa) believed themselves to be the "people of the sun," descended directly from Inti himself. The great Temple of the Sun at Coricancha is dedicated to this god. He is married to Mama Kilya, the moon goddess.

⚔ Mama Cocha ⚔
ALSO Cochamama

Mama Cocha was the goddess of the sea and fish. Sometimes depicted as a whale.

⚔ Manco Capac ⚔

Although not born a god, Manco Capac (the first Inca ruler) was blessed by the hand of Viracocha himself and is considered the earthly embodiment of the god (like the Hindu avatars). Future emperors considered themselves divine descendants of the sun god Inti. Manco Capac's mate was Mama Ocllo, and the two of them were reportedly the only beings who were allowed to survive the great flood that Viracocha unleashed upon the earth. It fell to them the duty to repopulate and civilize the earth. They learned the rules of civilization from Inti.

⚔ Mama Ocllo/Oello/Ogllo ⚔

The mother goddess, Mama Ocllo taught the art of spinning and weaving to the Inca people. She is the consort of Manco Capac, the first Inca ruler.

⚔ Pariacaca ⚔

Pariacaca is the god of rain and water; many Incan cities had large fountains to honor this god. He was born a falcon, then transformed into human form.

⚔ Quilla/Mama Kilya ⚔

Quilla is the moon goddess, goddess of marriage, and defender of women. She is the sister/wife of Inti the sun god.

⚱ Supay ⚱

God of death, Supay ruled the underworld (the *Uca Pacha*). The Inca strongly believed in an afterlife as much as the Egyptians did. (This parallel belief system drove Thor Heyerdahl to another expedition, wherein he and a crew sailed a boat made from Egyptian reeds across the Atlantic in an attempt to prove that the Egyptians may have arrived in the New World well before the Europeans, and influenced pre-Columbian civilizations living there. The expedition made it to within 600 miles (966 kilometers) of Central America.) The Inca practiced ritual mummification of their rulers; instead of burying them in elaborate tombs, the mummies were left in the palaces of their former lives. On certain holidays and for particular state functions, the mummies were dressed in their finest ceremonial regalia and paraded through the streets to receive their proper adulation. The mummies were among the most important of the sacred huacas.

⚱ Viracocha ⚱

Viracocha is the creator god is worshiped as a god of the ruling classes. The common people had other gods to turn to for their daily needs. Temples were built and dedicated to Viracocha in Cusco, as well as other cities; many sacrifices were made to him, particularly of the important llama, but also human sacrifices—including children. In Inca art, the god is frequently depicted as an old man with a long beard, leaning against a walking stick. At the ruins of Tiwanaku, Viracocha is portrayed as holding thunderbolts in both hands and wearing a crown with the rays of the sun shooting from it. The god weeps here, and his tears are said to depict the rains. The Spanish reported (and subsequently removed) a statue of Viracocha at Cusco sculpted at three-quarter scale from solid gold.

INCAN MYTHICAL MONSTERS

There were so many deities in Inca mythology that there doesn't seem to have been room for very many monsters—that, or the Inca simply weren't afraid of very much. However, there are plenty of other Latino monsters to keep kids in line. Here are some.

⊨ Ao Ao ⊨
Guarani

Ao Ao is a sheep- or monkey-like monster with huge fangs who has a love of eating humans. He gets his name from the howling noise he makes as he chases his victims—who can only escape his pursuit by climbing up a palm tree (which magically repels the creature).

⊨ El Culebrón ⊨
Chile

A monstrous anaconda with the head of a calf, El Culebrón emerges from caves and remote forests at night to devour anything in its path. It also has a mystical "radar" that allows it to discover buried treasure within forty days of internment. If you want to take the treasure from El Culebrón, try soaking the ground around it with sweet liqueur and hope that the drunken beast drops its guard long enough for you to dig up the riches.

⊨ El Sombrerón ⊨
Guatemala

A dwarfish man wearing a huge hat and black clothing and accessorized with fancy boots and buckles, he is an unpleasant—and typically unwanted—pursuer of women. To lure a woman, he stakes a string of mules in front of a her house, and then he serenades her until she comes outside; he then captures her and takes her to his home, where he feeds her dirt. He is drawn to have long hair, and is known to braid the manes and tails of horses for fun. A woman can protect herself from his unwanted pursuit by cutting her hair short.

⊰ Jasy Jatere/Yasy Yatere ⊱
Guarani

Similar to the Boogeyman, or to the Spanish El Cuco, this being targets naughty children who aren't properly taking a nap during their siesta. Non-napping children are lured into the forest, captured, and fed to Jasy Jatere's brother, Ao Ao. Jasy Jatere is an important deity in Guarani mythology: god of the siesta, guardian of yerba mate, and protector of hidden treasure. *Yerba mate* is a plant from the holly family native to South America. Its leaves are dried and used to make a potent tea with the same amount of caffeine as a cup of coffee, but also containing minerals and enzymes that are beneficial and help increase awareness and stamina. Jasy Jatere appears as a short man with long blond hair and blue eyes, carrying a staff.

⊰ Kurupi ⊱
Guarani

Kurupi is a small, ugly, hairy man with a prehensile penis that is so long he wears it wrapped several times around his waist. Women may blame unexpected pregnancies on a nighttime visit from him. Kurupi is the spirit of fertility and overt sexuality.

⊰ La Patasola ⊱
Columbia

A grotesque one-legged female vampire from the plains of Columbia, La Patasola is hideously ugly and hides her face behind stringy matted hair. She was cursed by being unfaithful to her husband and (thereby) dishonoring her children. She moves fast, despite her handicap, and is said to hop about while shrieking and wailing with grief. Rage drives her pursuit of male victims, who she lures by shape-shifting into the form of a beautiful woman; she can also assume the forms of various animal species.

⚜ Luison/Lobizón ⚜
Guarani

Luison resembles a werewolf and lurks in cemeteries in order to partake of rotting flesh. The stench of death is always around him. He is believed to be the lord of death, and a touch from him signifies impending doom. As Luison was the seventh son, it is considered bad luck to be born a seventh son lest the child carry the werewolf curse.

⚜ Massacooramaan/Masacurraman ⚜
Guyana

Massacooramaan is a huge, hairy monster of the rivers and seas that makes a habit of attacking and eating people who are traveling the waters in small boats. It was originally a *jumbee* (evil spirit) of Caribbean folklore, brought to the area by slaves imported to work the sugar cane fields.

⚜ Mbói Tu'i ⚜
Guarani

He is a serpent with the head of a parrot (his name means "snake parrot"). He has a blood-red forked tongue, scaly skin, and a feather-covered head from which he can emit a powerful "SQUAWK!" that can be heard from far away and strikes terror in those who hear it. He is lord-master of waterways and creatures of the water; he protects wetlands and all marine creatures.

⚜ Moñái ⚜
Guarani

He is also serpent-bodied, but has two horns on top of his reptilian head that act as antennae, and has the power to hypnotize his prey so that he can kill them easily. He is a trickster with a love of treasure, and he is often blamed when valuable things go missing.

⚔ Pishtaco ⚔
Peru, Bolivia

This creature is a mythological representation of the European invasion of South America in the 1500s. Pishtaco is a pale-skinned vampiric monster that kills native people to drain them of their body fat. In the sixteenth century, a Spanish priest recorded an increasing fear among the indigenous peoples of the time concerning the notion that the Spaniards were going to kill them and drain their body fat. It is quite possible that this idea arose from the very real experience of contracting "wasting diseases" from the Europeans (plague, cholera, measles, etc.) and becoming emaciated, and dying by the thousands.

⚔ Teju Jagua ⚔
Guarani

He is a lizard-like beast with the head of a dog and eyes of flame. Fortunately, he is slow-moving and mild-mannered. He is a cave spirit that eats and guards various fruits.

⚔ Yacumama ⚔
Peru, Ecuador

Yacumama is the mother of all sea monsters—literally. This monster is said to be over 150 feet (46 meters) in length, with a horned head and a territorial nature. Native peoples would sometimes blow a horn loudly before entering unknown waters (especially the Amazon River) to warn the beast of approaching humans. Allegedly, this would give the serpent time to move out of the area, but really it just sounds like a way of announcing lunch time.

As in the discussion of Mexican mythology earlier in this book, it must be mentioned that the arrival of the Europeans in South America had every bit the devastating impact upon the people and the cultures there that it did farther north. Along with the decimation of the indigenous tribes due to disease, slavery, and starvation, the introduction of Christianity forever changed the belief systems of the natives.

While Inca conquerors allowed native peoples to continue to follow their own beliefs (as long as they put the Inca gods *first*), Europeans declared native religions "heretical" and "blasphemous," and they were determined to eliminate the old gods completely. Due to the remoteness of some of the tribes (especially those in the Andes and extreme south of the continent), not all native belief systems were eradicated. From those that remained (and from carefully picking over the extremely biased accounts of the Spanish priests who worked with the native peoples), scholars have gleaned a fair understanding of indigenous mythology.

SOUTH AMERICAN SUPERSTITIONS

Here are some South American superstitions.

DREAMING ABOUT YOUR teeth falling out means there will be a death in the family.

DON'T PUT YOUR purse or wallet on the floor lest you lose all your money.

IN ADDITION TO black cats being unlucky, sleeping with a cat (or dog) will make you infertile.

ANYONE WHO STARES too long at a newborn can cast the evil eye upon it; give the baby a special bracelet (*azabache*) or necklace to prevent this.

SWEEPING A SINGLE woman's feet with a broom will prevent her from ever getting married.

DECORATING YOUR HOME with sea shells is bad luck. Evil spirits can hide inside the shells.

DON'T SCRATCH THAT itchy palm! Stick it in your pocket because money is coming your way.

IF YOU CUT a baby's hair before it learns to walk, it will delay the child's first steps. Cut it before they learn to *talk* and they never will!

A FULL GLASS of water on top of the refrigerator will absorb negative energy from evil spirits or nasty visitors and keep the home happy.

RINGING IN THE ears means someone's talking about you. To negate any malice they might spread, bite your tongue.

GLUE A PIECE of bread to the ceiling or above a door to ward off evil spirits.

WEARING RED PANTIES on New Year's Eve will help you find your soulmate, and bring good luck.

LOUDLY BANGING POTS and pans together brings good luck, too.

PUT A BUNCH of pennies under the carpets in a new home to bring good luck and healthy finances.

EATING A MANGO with milk will kill you.

THE SYMBOL OF an elephant with its trunk in the air brings financial wealth. (Curiously, there are no elephants in South America!)

DON'T GO BAREFOOT in the house or you'll catch a cold.

IF THE FIRST butterfly you see in the spring is white, you'll have luck all year.

CUTLERY IS MYSTICAL, and dropping a knife on the floor means a fight will start; drop a fork and a male visitor will come to your home; drop a spoon and the visitor will be female.

WEAR WHITE ON New Year's Eve for good luck. Since this is the middle of summer in South America, it would also be a cool and comfortable outfit.

A CHUNK OF rock salt in the corner of a room will drive away demons. In other parts of the world, salt is also used to deter—or contain—demons and ghosts.

EUROPE

Readers of this book will likely be most familiar with European culture. The imperialism of European countries ushered in the "Age of Discovery," which spread white Christian beliefs around the world—often with brutal imposition of those beliefs upon the local populace. The effects of such practices led to the homogenization of many unique cultures, and the destruction of a number of others. So, while European mythology has benefitted from exposure to many and varied religions and cultures, much of the variety and originality of those same cultures has disappeared all together. Still, European mythology remains the source of most familiar tales and traditions in Western civilization.

O f all the continents we've looked at so far in this book, perhaps none is quite so familiar as the mythology of Europe. The most powerful and iconic of evil beings find their origins in the folklore and religions of this long-settled region. Europe can be broadly divided into western and eastern halves, with eastern Europe dwarfing its western cousin in both land and area and total population. Eastern Europe, however, is one of the very few areas of the world that actually is experiencing negative population growth.

EASTERN EUROPE

The heavy-hitter in terms of both size and population here is Russia. While two-thirds of the land mass of Russia sits physically on the Asian continent, two-thirds of the population resides in the smaller portion of the country that sits on the European continent. For this reason, Russia is considered to be a European nation. Thus, Russia's contribution to the mythology and folklore of the entire continent of Europe cannot be overstated.

Russian folklore basically has two major influences: the pagan religious beliefs and superstitions of the ancient Slavic peoples, as well as the stories and beliefs that arose following the adoption of Orthodox Christianity and/or Roman Catholicism. The Slavs were semi-nomadic peoples of the steppes, who were divided into tribes (in much the same way as peoples of North America) based on religious beliefs and practices as well as cultural differences. Uncovering the mythologies of the Slavs is difficult since the tribes were historically illiterate, instead passing along their knowledge and stories through oral tradition. What has been written down may be greatly changed by the filter of Orthodox Christianity that the scribes and priests practiced.

Slavic religions all seem to be based in the same general polytheistic paganism that was shared across the prehistoric peoples of Europe. The differences were usually localized, and typically resulted in different gods from the mutual pantheon being given prominence by various tribes. The Slavs eventually became clustered under three broad categories: Eastern Slavs (Russians, Belarussians, and Ukrainians), Western Slavs (Czechs, Slovaks, Poles, and Sorbs), and Southern Slavs (Serbs, Croats, Slovenes, and Bulgarians).

EASTERN EUROPEAN GODS AND GODDESSES

Because of the extended period of human habitation and the frequent intermingling of tribes, Eastern European gods and goddesses have multiple names and talents.

⚜ BELOBOG ⚜
ALSO BYELOBOG, BELABOG, BIELOBOG, BIELEBOG, BILOBOG, BELUN

Slavic god of goodness, light, luck, and happiness, he is the white god to Chernobog's black god moniker. The two are locked in eternal combat for the kingship of the universe.

⚜ CHERNOBOG ⚜

Originally a minor deity, Chernobog grew in notoriety to become the god of evil. Chernobog became evil when he succumbed to the temptations of the world; his mind was overtaken by the injustices of life and by the depression and anger that resulted. He was known for murdering people by smashing in their heads with his huge hammer. He is also called "the black god" because of his evil—and because he turned himself into a giant black serpent and slid over the earth, corrupting the hearts of men. This act began the war with Svarog.

⚜ Dažbog ⚜
also Dazhbog, and other spellings

Dažbog is one of the three members of the *Triglav*, the Slavic "holy trinity" (together with Perun and Svarog). The Triglav has three silver heads stacked one atop the other, representing the sky, the earth, and the underworld. Dažbog was created by Svarog to aid in that god's battle against the evil Chernobog. Sometimes referred to as Svarog's son, he is god of solar heat (the "fire of heaven"), the rain, and the underworld. *Dažd*, in a number of Slavic languages, means "rain." He is also the founder of the Slavic peoples. Southern Slavs (especially Serbs) refer to Dažbog as "lame Daba," who is depicted as an old man who wears a bear skin and leans on a staff. Lame Daba is nearly always in the company of a wolf, and the wolf is sacred to Serbs. To Christian Serbs, Lame Daba is an evil god of the underworld, akin to Satan.

⚜ Dodola ⚜

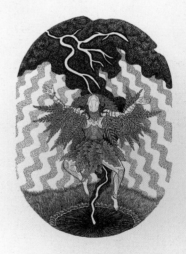

Goddess of rain and wife of Perun, she brings about rain by milking her heavenly cows, causing the milk to fall upon the earth. She is tricked by Veles (who is jealous of Perun and wants whatever that god has) into sniffing a lily-of-the-valley blossom, whereupon she immediately falls unconscious. She spontaneously gives birth to a son—and since Veles has no wife or children, he decides to take the boy and raise him as his own. When Perun learns of this, he wages war against Veles for three days and three nights, finally emerging victorious. Afterwards, he banishes Veles to the underworld, where Veles becomes a giant serpent.

⚜ Domovoi and Kikimora ⚜

These are male and female (respectively) "house spirits," similar to brownies and gnomes of Western European myth, which reside in human homes. These spirits are not inherently "good" or "evil," but their cooperation can generally be secured by respecting them, and giving them small offerings of food and cloth. They, in turn, will keep lesser malevolent spirits away and keep the household running smoothly.

⚜ Hors ⚜

Hors is an Eastern Slavic deity, god of the winter sun; he may have originated from contact with Turkish and Iranian peoples as his name stems from an old Persian word meaning "sun." It was believed that Hors was killed each spring by Chernobog and replaced with the summer sun; he rose again when the short days of winter returned.

⚜ Koschei the Immortal ⚜

More of a Russian demi-god than a god, Koschei is immortal because his vulnerable soul is hidden inside a needle—which is inside an egg, which is inside a rabbit, which is locked inside an iron chest, which is buried beneath an oak tree, which grows on an island. In other words, good luck killing this guy. He enjoys riding his horse around naked and kidnapping women.

⚜ Kremara ⚜
also Kremata
Lithuanian

Kremara is the god of butchering pigs. He teams up with Priparchis (god of nurturing baby pigs) to ensure that the animals are healthy and happy—then he cleanly and humanely butchers them.

⚜ Mokosh ⚜
Mat Zemlya, also Mokoš, Mokos, Mokusa, Makosh

Mokosh is the earth goddess herself, Mother Nature; she may also have been responsible for protecting women (especially those in labor), and for sponsoring the feminine arts of spinning, weaving, and sewing.

⚜ Morana ⚜

Morana is the goddess of winter and death. During the celebration of spring, an effigy of Morana was ritually burned and/or drowned to end winter and usher in the season of rebirth.

⚜ Perun ⚜

The second of the two primary Eastern Slavic gods, Perun was constantly enraged by Veles' actions, and spent much of his time trying to kill Veles with lightning bolts (Perun's name means "lightning" in various Slavic languages). Perun is god of the sky, and master of wind, fire, and lightning. He allegedly wielded an axe that would return to his hand boomerang-style after it was thrown. It is interesting to note that a number of Slavic myths have similarities to Nordic myths (such as the boomeranging weapons of Thor and Perun). It is possible that these mythologies were spread through contact with—or even evolution from—far-ranging Celtic tribes (Keltoi, to the Greeks), whose archaeological remains have been discovered as far away as China.

⚜ Samodiva ⚜
also samovila, vila, veela
see entry for [The] Vile

Samodiva are the fairy folk of Serbian and Bulgarian folklore. The Vila Samodiva is a beautiful fairy maiden who acts as the go-between for the fairy realm and mortal men. She may task the hero who contacts her in order to test his valor. It is she who leads the other *vile* (plural of *vila*) in their dances, and protects them from harm—sometimes using her power over fire. Those who witness the dancing often fall under its spell and join in, only to perish from exhaustion before the coming dawn. The origins of the vile may be in Thrace (an ancient land north of Greece), whose people would have been in contact with the Slavs. Vile are typically described as beautiful women with long blonde hair.

⚔ SIMARGL ⚔

Simargl was an Eastern Slavic deity and god of grain—especially barley (which is grown to make beer). He may have originated from contact with Turkish and Iranian peoples, and his name can be translated as "barley" or "harvest." He was also created by Svarog to aid in the war against Chernobog. He is usually depicted as a dog (or sometimes a lion) with wings. (See entry under *The Zorya* on the next page.)

⚔ SVANTEVIT ⚔

Svantevit is the four-faced god of war, abundance, divination, and fertility. Svantevit is the well-known god of Western Slavs—and possibly Ukraine as well. Each face represents one of the cardinal directions: north, east, south, and west.

⚔ SVAROG ⚔

Svarog is the creator god (depending on the researcher) and top god of the Slavic pantheon. He is described as the "assistant" to the creator god Rod. Svarog is the personification of the sky, and the fire that originated there. He is the archetypal blacksmith (like the Roman Vulcan), but in the sky rather than the underworld.

⚔ SVAROŽIĆ ⚔
"SON OF SVAROG"

The suffix -žić can be translated as "little" or "baby." It is generally attached to the names of children who are named for someone still living—though not always someone who is related to the children.

⚔ [The] Vile ⚔

Slavic "fairies" are wicked little creatures who can allegedly kill a person by causing him to "dance" to death. They are even known to tickle people so long that they die of asphyxiation due to laughing. Even their screams could kill!

⚔ Veles ⚔

One of two major Eastern Slavic gods, Veles was a serpentine beast of underground origin who was said to rule the earth, water, and magic. He was devious, but not exactly evil, with a taste for stealing the possessions of his nemesis, Perun. Veles was also the guardian of cattle.

⚔ Yarilo/Yarovit ⚔

Slavic patron god of the harvest, vegetation, and fertility, he was the son born to Dodola, Perun's wife, when Veles tricked her into sniffing the lily-of-the-valley flower. The kidnapping of Yarilo was the cause of Veles to be banished from the heavens to the underworld.

⚔ [The] Zorya ⚔

These are the Three Star Sisters. They are Slavic goddesses of the sun, each with her own duties. Zorya Utrennyaya is goddess of the dawn who lets the sun out of Dažbog's home each day to make its trip across the sky. Zorya Vechernyaya is goddess of the evening who closes the door behind the sun after it returns home at sunset. Zorya (the nameless) is the embodiment of midnight. In addition to their sun duties, the Zorya must carefully guard the fierce dog that is imprisoned in the constellation Ursa Minor. The dog (or sometimes a bear) is Simargl in his animal form; he strains against his chains in order to be free to wreak havoc across the universe.

Eastern European Mythical Monsters

Some of the most fantastical and intricate magical beasts and monsters come from this region.

⊰ Baba Yaga ⊱
Western Russia

Not a specific witch, but rather a "species" of witch, Baba Yaga lives in the forest in a magical cottage that stands on chicken feet. Baba Yaga can fly through the air by use of a floating mortar and pestle, which grinds the herbs for their magic spells. Baba Yaga have teeth made of iron, and noses so long they can touch the roof of the cottage. The cottage is topped with the head of a rooster—maybe the same one that donated its feet for the cottage to stand on—and surrounded by a fence of human bones. These witches are (understandably) considered primarily evil, but their good will can be bought and their aid can be attributed to to an individual's cause. They might also take up the cause of a person just because they wish to.

⊰ Baubai ⊱
Lithuania

Baubai (singular Baubas) are Lithuanian "boogeymen" who hide in dark corners and spaces in the house, waiting to take naughty children away with them.

⊰ Brosnya ⊱
Western Russia

In Lake Brosno there is said to live a giant beast with the head of a dragon and a long, thin trailing tail. Comparisons to the Loch Ness monster abound, with some saying the two are related. There is speculation that this creature was responsible for the hasty retreat of the Mongol-Tater army from the area in the eighth century CE. It seems that they encountered a giant creature that ate horses and unlucky soldiers.

⊰ Hastrman ⊱
Poland

A creature of Polish myth, the Hastrman is an equal-opportunity consumer of both children *and* adults. He walks along river banks on full-moon nights and cries like a lost child, causing people to rush to him. He's also a cat-lover and has a cart pulled by felines. When he's not eating people, he is said to knit clothes for the souls of those he consumed.?

⊰ Kraconach ⊱
Poland and Czech Republic

A Yeti-like beast that lives in the mountains between Poland and the Czech Republic, Kraconach's moods can swing from wanting to eat everyone and everything in sight, to acting as a helpful finder of lost hikers.

⊰ Krampus ⊱
Germany/Western Russia

With its origin unknown, Krampus is the antithesis of Santa Claus. While Santa rewards good little children with presents and candy, Krampus punishes bad little children by whipping them with birch branches. If the children are especially naughty, Krampus will stuff them in his sack and carry them off to his lair—never to be seen again. Krampus is usually depicted as a demonic half-goat, half-man creature.

⊰ Pricolici ⊱
Romania

A Romanian monster, Pricolici is said to be the soul of an evil man that animates the body of a wolf, very similar to a werewolf/vampire hybrid. Its reason for living is to create chaos and do harm. The creatures are enormous, and are reported to be extra fond of holy men and priests.

⚔ RARACH ⚔
CZECH REPUBLIC

Known by many names, these nasty things are a type of "rogue" house spirit that has lost its desire to be helpful. Sometimes benign, but frequently dangerous, they are often the force behind household "accidents" that could turn fatal (falling down the stairs, cutting yourself with a knife, etc.).

⚔ RUSALKI ⚔
RUSSIA

Rusalki (singular Rusalka) are fish-like or mermaid-like women who inhabit the waters of Russia. They are said to be the spirits of women who either committed suicide or who were murdered by their lovers. Rusalki can lure gullible men to a watery death by singing, and then pulling them into the water (frequently by entangling the men in their hair and drowning them). The first full week of June is celebrated as "Rusalka Week" in Russia, and is said to be the time when the creatures are most active. Rusalki appear as beautiful but eerie women who are soaking wet, with water actively streaming from their hair and off of their bodies. They are generally found in lakes, ponds, and rivers, as opposed to urban water sources.

⚔ STRIGOI ⚔
ROMANIA

These are hideous creatures of Romanian myth, which may have given rise to the vampire. Strigoi are shape-shifters who can assume any form they wish—or become invisible to attack their human prey and drink their blood. They come in two different varieties: living (Strigoi Viu, which are like witches or vampires) and undead (Strigoi Mort, which have risen from the grave). Strigoi arise through various means: a person who dies before they marry, a child born with a caul, or someone whose dead body was walked on by a cat can all become strigoi. They reportedly have red hair, blue eyes—and two hearts. They can shape-shift into animal forms to get close to people in order to drink their blood. It is from these creatures that Hollywood devised the various ways to kill vampires: a stake through the heart, sunlight, and garlic are all capable of taking down Strigoi.

⚔ URIAS ⚔
RUSSIA

An example of post-Christian mythology, the Urias were a race of giants that were the first people to inhabit the earth. They were said to have lived peacefully with humans when humanity first appeared, but they eventually caused war and conflict until God flooded the earth—saving only Noah, his family, and the animals on the ark. Biblical giants are described in the Old Testament (in Genesis and elsewhere) as being from "the sons of God and the daughters of humans." The term used is *nephilim*, which has been translated as "giants" or, alternatively, as "the fallen." So, giants both pre-date humanity and yet are a result of matings between angels and human women. Romanian mythology states that one can find buried treasure by seeking out the burial sites of Urias on the high holy days of Christmas Eve, Easter, and Saint George's Day (April 23 on the Orthodox calendar). You will know these burial sites by the fires burning atop them.

⚔ VAMPIRE/VAMPYR ⚔
ROMANIA

The most famous of all monsters, this Romanian nightmare creature rises from the earth each night to stalk the land and drink the blood of its helpless victims. Hollywood has glamourized the creatures to the point that they have become romantic objects desired by thousands of swooning teenage girls. Originally, these fiends reeked of death and the blood they consumed, were able to shape-shift at will, and could only be killed by the ritualistic driving of a wooden stake through their bodies to pin them into their graves, followed by cutting their heads from their bodies and burning them.

The legend of the vampire may have arisen from fear of some of the warlords of ancient times. Many of these overlords were rumored to be hideously cruel to their tenant farmers, taking all of their possessions to pay exorbitant taxes and murdering those who were unable to pay. The notorious Vlad T,epes—also Vlad the Impaler, or Vlad Dracula—was the basis for Bram Stoker's undead creature. T,epes was rumored to be excessively cruel to the Transylvanian Saxons who opposed him, killing them all by having stakes driven through their bodies from throat through opposite end, and then displaying the impaled corpses outside of his castle. Transylvanians rewarded this behavior by (figuratively) turning Dracula into a mythical monster. Later, T,epes attacked armies of Ottoman Turks and Bulgarians, slaughtering them by the tens of thousands.

⊰ VLADIMIR LEDENEV ⊱
RUSSIA

Poor Vladimir is a kind of urban legend. His mummified remains were found inside his apartment *six years* after he unexpectedly went missing. It seems that no one had bothered to actually check out Vlad's apartment, but instead had simply knocked on the door then walked away when he didn't answer. Meanwhile, Vlad was moldering on the other side of the door. When he was finally found, he was allegedly sitting at his kitchen table with an empty bottle of vodka in front of him.

⊰ VODYANOY ⊱
RUSSIA

Once again demonstrating the primal fear of water, Vodyanoy is a frogish beast that lives alone in bodies of water and acts to drown people. This creature is particularly linked with Christianity, carrying out his murderous mission on those who dare to swim on holy days, who forget to make the sign of the cross before taking a dip, or who have the audacity to swim after sunset.

⊰ ZMEYS ⊱
SLOVAKIA

Zmeys (singular Zmey) are mythical dragons of Eastern and Southern Slavs. They don't defend hoards of treasure like European dragons frequently do, but they are known to own palaces and have great wealth sequestered in far-off lands. They can speak and breathe fire, as well as shape-shift into human form. They can be appeased with large offerings of gold—or by the gift of young maidens. Oh, and they often have multiple heads. Romanians call these dragons *belaurs*.

EASTERN EUROPEAN SUPERSTITIONS

In general, Eastern Europeans tend to be more superstitious than their Western counterparts; 50 percent of Russian people in a recent poll admitted that they modified their behavior to conform to superstitious or magical beliefs. Here are some interesting superstitions.

DON'T WEAR CLOTHES inside out. Doing so raises the risk of you getting beaten up. If you do so accidentally—but then immediately fix them to right-side out again—you can escape a thrashing if you ask someone to whack you on the back.

FLOWERS MUST ONLY be gifted in odd numbers; so, your bouquet can have thirteen flowers but not twelve. Giving even-numbered flowers will put off the recipient, seeing as Russians only take even numbers of flowers to cemeteries.

IF YOU'RE TO the halfway point on a journey, do not turn around and go back home or ill luck will befall you. If you forgot something vital and you *must* return, look in a mirror before leaving the house and resuming your journey.

NEVER SHAKE HANDS over a threshold (also never hug or kiss over it). There's a house spirit that lives there, and your actions in his space might disturb him—and that's a bad idea. Instead, step inside the house, then make your greetings.

SIMILAR TO SOME Chinese gifts, giving certain household objects can be problematic. For example, giving an object with a sharp edge (like a knife or scissors) can lead to arguments with the recipient. It's possible to avoid this by charging the recipient a ruble for the gift, thereby turning it into a "sale" and changing its nature. Gifting a handkerchief can cause tears, while gifting an empty purse is bad luck. A purse should have a coin or other monetary amount in it so that the recipient is never poor.

SIT BETWEEN TWO people with the same name to get lucky. Popular names are very common in Russia, so if there are two Ivans or two Natashas at a party, get between them and make a wish and it will come true. Of course, don't tell anyone what you wished for.

SALTY FOOD MEANS that the cook has fallen in love, so don't complain about it.

DON'T LICK A knife. Doing so will turn you into an evil person (likely a liar, since we know that liars have split tongues!).

IF SOMEONE WISHES you "good luck," your reply must be "to heck with that!" or some version of such. Thanking someone for wishing you luck will cause misfortune. Other versions of this myth state that the first person should never actually say "good luck," but instead should say the Russian equivalent of "no fur, no feathers," to which you would give the same "to heck with that!" response. In a similar fashion, performers traditionally say "break a leg" to each other before going on stage to ensure a good performance.

NEVER LEAVE EMPTY bottles on the table. Whether your party's tab is determined by the number of empties, or you're following the tradition of finishing every bottle that is opened, empties should be put on the floor beneath the table.

ALL MEMBERS OF a traveling party must sit down together briefly before moving on. This ensures that everyone will have a safe trip.

"KNOCK ON WOOD" is big in Russia. They don't say it out loud, and they mime spitting over their left shoulder three times (symbolically spitting in the devil's eye). If there's no wood around, they'll knock on their own heads.

IF YOU ACCIDENTALLY step on someone's foot, expect your own to get stepped on as well. It is believed that returning the same offense to the offender prevents any future fights between you.

DO NOT WALK on opposite sides of a pole if you are with a friend or loved one. Doing so means that the relationship will end! Make sure that both of you pass a pole on the *same* side.

HICCUPS MEAN SOMEONE is thinking about you.

WHISTLING INDOORS IS very bad luck, and it can lead to you losing all your money.

SINGLE PEOPLE SHOULD never sit at the corner of a table, or they will never get married. Children are exempted from this.

NEVER SIT DIRECTLY on the [cold] ground because it will make you infertile. This rule is particularly true for women. Sitting on a blanket or other ground cover is ok.

NEVER WISH SOMEONE a happy birthday before the actual date, lest misfortune befall them. Likewise, don't celebrate your own birthday before the actual date.

WESTERN EUROPE

While Western Europe is dwarfed by its Eastern brother, it has played a major—if not *the* major—role in determining the governance of the nations of the world. Western Europe (including subdivisions of Southern and Central Europe) contains the countries of Austria, Belgium, Croatia, the Czech Republic, Denmark, Estonia, Finland, France, Germany, Hungary, Ireland, Italy, Liechtenstein, Luxembourg, Monaco, the Netherlands, Norway, Poland, Portugal, Slovakia, Slovenia, Spain, Sweden, Switzerland, and the United Kingdom—and sometimes (depending on which governing body is defining it) the smaller nations of Andorra, Greece, Iceland, Latvia, Lithuania, Malta, Monaco, and San Marino. The Republic of

Turkey is actually transcontinental, with the greater portion of it residing on the continent of Asia.

Christianity is far and away the predominant religion in Western Europe, with over 70 percent of the population identifying themselves as Christian. Following the "Great Schism" of 1054 CE, the Christian world was divided into Western Christianity (Catholic or Protestant religions that use the Latin alphabet) and Eastern Christianity (Orthodox religions that use the Greek or Cyrillic alphabets). Dividing Europe along strictly religious lines is problematic for countries like Greece, which is overwhelmingly Orthodox, but is practically never included in what would be called Eastern Europe, for various reasons.

Also, because of the influence of the former USSR, countries like Hungary, East Germany, Poland, and Romania came to be associated with Eastern Europe and Russia rather than with the West (and the so-called "Western Bloc" countries that were divided by their loyalties during the Cold War). Religion (which is the source of most mythology) in Western Europe was historically Catholic, until the rise of Protestantism in the sixteenth century. Prior to this, religious zealotry was frequent, and included the scourge of the Spanish Inquisition, as well as religious wars such as the Crusades.

CELTIC GODS AND GODDESSES

The ancient Celts weren't limited to the British Isles, but instead spread across vast tracks of Europe and Asia, taking their art and cultural influences to people as far away as China.

ÁINE

Goddess of love, summer, wealth, and kingship, she is sometimes represented by a red mare and is referred to as a fairy queen, a sun or a moon goddess, and goddess of abundant harvests. She is an ancient goddess who has taken on many different aspects through the centuries. She is the Lady of the Lake in Arthurian myth, Mother Nature and goddess of the earth, and goddess of magic and luck (the embodiment of the "luck of the Irish"). Her history is complex, but she has strong ties to County Limerick and County Munster. Some even see her as an aspect of the Morrígan.

⚜ Allfadir ⚜
Franks

As an omnipotent "all father" of several Frankish tribes and generally associated with Wuotan/Wodin/Odin, Allfadir is the supreme deity of Norse myth. "All Father" is another of Odin's epithets. Allfadir was believed to reside in clumps of sacred oaks, and sacrifices of game animals—and perhaps humans—were made on altars to him in those groves.

⚜ Aos si/Aes sídhe ⚜
Ireland/Scotland

These are supernatural beings similar to elves and fairies. The term *sidhe* (or *sìth*, in Scottish Gaelic) means "mounds" and refers to the belief that these beings live in earthen mounds underground.

⚜ Belenus ⚜
Italy

Belenus (spellings vary) is the ancient god of the sun who is still celebrated during the neo-pagan festivals of Beltane (May Day), which mark the start of summer. He is strongly associated with horses, and he may be affiliated with the Greco-Roman god Apollo, who drove his shining chariot of the sun across the sky each day.

⚜ Brigid/Brigit ⚜
Ireland

Goddess of hand-to-hand combat, poetry, healing, smithing, chickens, farmhands, single mothers, and cowherds (among other things), she is the fiery and highly popular daughter of Dagda. She survived the arrival of Christianity by becoming Saint Bridget.

⚜ Cernunnos ⚜
Gaul

Cernunnos is the god of fertility, animals, and life; Cernunnos is the Horned God, which may have been the model for the Christian devil. With his horned head and cloven feet, Cernunnos represents the wildness of nature and the "undisciplined" aspects of humanity. To Christians, he is an example of what can become of you if you don't pay strict attention to the tenets of the faith.

⌁ CREDNE/CREIDHNE ⌁
IRELAND

Credne is a smith of precious metals for the Tuatha Dé Danann. Together with his brothers Goibniu and Luchtaine, he formed the trinity known as the Trí Dée Dána (the three gods of art), who forged the magical weapons the Tuatha Dé Danann used against the Fomorians. He is frequently confused with Creidne, a female warrior of Irish myth.

⌁ DAGDA ⌁
ALSO DAGDHA, AN DAGDA, EOCHAID-OLLATHAIR
IRELAND

Dagda is the first king of the Tuatha Dé Danann; he is god of war, death, feasting, and magic. A hearty being with an enormous appetite, he is said to own a giant cauldron of stew that never empties and a roasting boar that never runs out of meat. His war club is so massive that it must be transported in a wheeled cart; the working end will kill you, but the handle can bring you back to life. He is generally jovial and hard-partying. Dagda is married to the Morrígan, and he fathered the war goddess, Brigit.

⌁ EPONA ⌁
GAUL

Epona is the goddess of horses, and one of the most ancient Celtic deities. The Celts used horses (as well as mules and donkeys, which likely performed the grudge work of plowing and bearing burdens) for agriculture, war, and traveling great distances, making the animals a crucial part of Celtic life. Epona is considered so powerful and important that even the invading Roman legions took up worship of her, to the extent of honoring her with her own feast day on the Roman calendar.

As she is often depicted with bread or grain (which might have been meant for feeding horses), she is thought to have been celebrated as a goddess of abundance and fertility as well.

⊰ Ériu ⊱
Ireland

Ériu is the matron goddess and namesake of the island of Éire (Ireland). Together with her sisters Banba and Fódla, she comprises a triumvirate of "sovereignty goddesses," who, by virtue of being the living embodiment of a territory, confer kingship of it on a husband or lover. Ériu and her sisters are queens of the *Tuatha Dé Danann*.

⊰ Lir ⊱
also Ler, Llyr
Ireland

An old Irish primordial sea god (the personification of the ocean), Lir fathered Manannán Mac Lir, who became god of the sea. A character who may or may not be the same, Lir suffered four of his children being changed into swans for nine hundred years in the Irish folktale *The Children of Lir*.

⊰ Lug/Lugh ⊱
also Lugh Lámfhota, or Lugh Lamfada
Ireland

God of the sunlight and handcrafts and chief god of Irish Celts, his name means "shining," and he is depicted as fair-haired and handsome. His invincible spear—which accompanies him everywhere—seems like an extension of his arm, giving him the nickname, "Hugh Long Arms." He is patron of almost everything, including music, magic, healing, harvest, and war. He is also the father of the legendary Irish hero, Cúchulainn.

Born of a union between a Fomorian woman and a man of the Tuatha Dé Danann, and raised as a foster by the great god of the sea, Manannán mac Lir, Lugh chose to help the Tuatha Dé Danann against their mortal enemies. It was Lugh who led the Fey folk against the Fomorians, killing his grandfather Balor (king of the

Fomorians) by shooting him in the eye with a slingshot and then cutting off Balor's head (note the similarity to the Biblical story of David and Goliath; the Fomorians were believed to be the sons of Ham, who was cursed by his father Noah).

Lugh is still celebrated during the traditional harvest festival of Lughnasadh (or Lughnasa).

⊰ MACHA ⊱
IRELAND

An Irish fertility goddess; the king of Ulster forced Macha to race against his horses while she was heavy with child. Despite this, she won and then cursed the men of Ulster to feel the pains of labor every time they went into battle. She is sometimes counted as one of the three faces of the Morrígan, and she is usually depicted with red hair.

⊰ MANANNÁN MAC LIR ⊱
IRELAND

Irish god of the sea and one of the founding members of the Tuatha Dé Danann, Manannán possessed a boat named *Scuabtuinne* ("wave sweeper"), which didn't need sails; a magical sword named Fragarach ("answerer" or "retaliator"), which could cut through any armor and which forced anyone to tell the truth when confronted with its point; a flaming helmet; and a "cloak of mist" that rendered him invisible. It was he who provided the mist (the féth fíada) that the Tuatha Dé Danann used to hide themselves from human sight, as well as the "feasting boar" that never ran out of meat (a similar creature was owned by Odin). He also owned a spotted cow that only gave milk that was honey-flavored and alcoholic (mead), as well as a number of other magical items. The highest-ranked god (after Dagda) in the pre-Christian pantheon, Manannán mac Lir transported the remaining Tuatha Dé Danann to the mysterious Otherworld (the *Sidhe*) following their defeat by the Milesian people. The Milesians were the first invading "mortals" to rule Ireland Manannán subsequently became god of the Underworld and protector of the Sidhe.

⚔ Medb ⚔
also Maeve, Meadhbh, Méabh
Ireland

Irish mother goddess and Queen of Connaught, her name means "intoxication" and doesn't only refer to drunkenness. She makes her suitors fall hopelessly in love with her, then makes them fight to the death. She famously prevailed in battle against the forces of Ulster—but was reduced in lore to simply Mab, Queen of the Fairies, following the arrival of Christianity.

⚔ [The] Morrígan ⚔
also Morríghan, Morrigu, Morrigna, Mór-Ríoghain
Ireland

Terrifying war goddess and beautiful mother goddess, the Morrígan is the most powerful goddess in Celtic myth. A founding member of the Tuatha Dé Danann, she always picks the winning side in any battle (perhaps her presence alone is enough to turn the tide!), and she is frequently joined in battle by her sisters, Badb and Nemain, who help her rip the enemy to pieces. The sisters are sometimes thought of as a trinity (a deity with three aspects), while in other discussions, the Morrígan's other faces seem to be Badb ("the war crow") and Macha. As a shape-shifter, the Morrígan has many aspects; her primary form is a battle crow, though she can also change from gorgeous woman to wizened hag. In the latter form, she is usually referred to as the Washer Woman or The Washer at the Ford (Bean Nighe); she terrifies the enemy by being seen washing their bloody uniforms in the nearest river, thus heralding their doom.

⚔ Ogma ⚔
also Ogham, Ogmious
Gaul

Battle god of Celtic myth, Ogma was the model for the Berserkers—legendary warriors who were driven insane by battle lust, and had to be restrained with leather straps or metal chains to keep them from rushing into battle too soon. Ogma was depicted as a huge swarthy man, mature of years, and armed with a war club and a bow or sword. He also may, surprisingly, have been a god of eloquence, gifted with glibness and wit to turn the hearts and minds of his foes. Some illustrations show a chain gang of men linked to the god's tongue and trailing behind him. The historic Ogham alphabet of Ireland was named for him.

⊰ TARANIS ⊱
GAUL, IRELAND, NORTHERN SPAIN

God of thunder, Taranis is very strongly associated with the wheel, which appears as a motif throughout Celtic-influenced lands. Taranis was folded into the mantle of Jupiter by the Romans. In Irish Gaelic, his name is Tuireann (various spellings), and it shares the same root as the Norse Thor and the Germanic Donar, both gods of thunder.

⊰ TUATHA DÉ DANANN ⊱
IRELAND

Currently described as the Fey, or the "fairy folk" of Ireland, the Tuatha Dé Danann were once considered gods and the ancestors of the Irish people. They are said to have arrived mysteriously in a cloud of mist from across the northern sea. Tuatha Dé Danann is said to mean "the children of Danu"; Danu was the ancient creator goddess of the earth. Together with her husband Donn—who would be turned into the oaken world tree that held up the heavens—she made the earth from a chunk of dry dirt that she watered with her copious tears.

The Tuatha Dé Danann were rich in magic and ancient power, which not only enabled them to overcome the Fomorians, but also established the Tuatha Dé Danann as gods among men. They brought with them from across the sea four deeply magical objects: Lia Fail, the Stone of Destiny (also the Stone of Scone, upon which ancient Irish—and later, Scottish—kings were crowned); the Invincible Spear of Lugh (which always hit its target mere moments after being thrown, and made Lugh unstoppable in battle); the "Shining Sword" of Nuada (also called the Sword of Light), which could allegedly dispel truth from lies, enforce the law, dispense justice, and punish the enemies of Ireland; and the Cauldron of Dagda, which not only continuously dispensed unlimited food and drink to the worthy, but was also capable of healing wounds and resurrecting dead warriors.

Tuatha Dé Danann were larger, stronger, and more beautiful than ordinary men, as well as highly skilled in the arts of music, crafts, language, and war—and magic. The Druids arose from them. They were also the last supernatural race of beings to rule Ireland; they were defeated by the Milesians—a race of mortals from northern Europe (also the Gaels, the true ancestors of the Irish people). Over time, the Tuatha Dé Danann became associated with the places they lived (the "mounds" above and below ground to which they retreat), and the term "the Sidhe" has come to refer to the beings themselves and not just the Otherworld.

GERMANIC GODS AND GODDESSES

Most of Germanic mythology derives from Western Russia and the ancient tribes of Central Europe, along with major influences from the Nordic people peoples of Sweden, Norway, and Denmark.

⊰ BALDER ⊱
ALSO BALDUR AND BALDR, THE "SHINING ONE"
NORSE

Balder is god of everything good: peace, innocence, and forgiveness. He was beautiful, kind, and universally loved—except by a jealous Loki. At his birth, Frigg made all the living things in existence swear an oath not to harm him. Unfortunately, she somehow missed the lowly mistletoe; it was by using a dart made from mistletoe—and the unsuspecting help of Balder's blind brother Hoder—that Loki brought about Balder's death. Despite attempts at resurrection, Balder remained dead, and Loki was captured and sentenced to eternal punishment.

⊰ EOSTRE ⊱
ALSO ĒOSTRE, OSTARA, EASTRE,
ĒASTRE, ESTHER, ISHTAR

The Anglo-Saxon goddess of fertility and life, Eostre is celebrated on the day of the Spring Equinox (usually March 21), often with a sacrifice of a young lamb or rabbit. Rabbits are sacred to her as symbols of abundant fertility (not bringers of chocolate), and eggs symbolize rebirth and renewal. The Christian holiday of Easter was superimposed on top of Eostre's feast day—even using Eostre's name—as one of a number of attempts to make Christianity more popular with pagans.

⚔ FREYA/FREYJA ⚔
NORSE

Goddess of love, fertility, and sex—and wife of the god Óð—these two are continuously being conflated with Frigg and Odin, and scholars are split on whether the two couples are actually versions of the same two gods. While Freya is described as "promiscuous," her husband is a wanderer, too; his yearly disappearances are explained as the season of winter, when the sun leaves the sky for months at a time.

⚔ FREYA ⚔
PERHAPS ALSO FRIGG

Freya is the Norse goddess of love and fertility, as well as a fierce fighter in her own right. As such, she is leader of the Valkyrie until she weds Odin. She owns a fabulous enchanted necklace called Brisingamen, made of golden amber, that has the power to make any man fall in love with her. It was stolen from her by Loki, but allegedly returned by Heimdall, watchman of the gods. She had daughters named Hnoss/Hnossa (goddess of infatuation and sensuality) and Gersemi (goddess of beauty).

⚔ FRIGE ⚔
ALSO FRIG, FRI, FRIJJŌ, FRĪJA, FRĪG, FRIKE,
FREKE, FRICK, FUIK, FREA

The Anglo-Saxon fertility goddess and wife of Woden, Frige predates Frigg, and was the model for that Norse goddess. Friday is named for her.

⚔ GAUT ⚔
ALSO GAUTR, GAUTAZ, GAUTI, GEAT,
GĒAT, GUTI, GOTHUS

Gaut is a Germanic ancestral deity who lent his name to the Goth and Visigoth ("Western Goths") tribes. They helped bring about the fall of the Roman Empire in the third and fourth centuries CE.

⊰ Heimdall ⊱
also Heimdallr, Gullintani

The Norse god of light, security, and seeing, he is guardian of the gods and of Bifrost, the Rainbow Bridge (also Bilfrost, Asabru, Asbru) that connects the Nine Realms. He is gifted with sight that is powerful enough to see into the Nine Realms, with hearing so acute it is said he can hear grass growing. The son of Odin (and allegedly nine different mothers *simultaneously*), he carries a magic horn named Gjail/Gjallar, which he will blow to sound the final battle when Ragnarök comes. He returnes Freya/Frigg's precious necklace Brisingamen to Asgard, but not to Freya. It is safely kept somewhere in Asgard.

⊰ Hel/Hela ⊱

Goddess of the Helheim, Hel is the only daughter of Loki. She is said to be a hideous hag, with gangrenous legs and blue skin. In the icy dampness of the Helheim, she rules over a bunch of apathetic wastrel souls who never performed deeds worthy of a place in Valhalla.

⊰ Hermod ⊱
also Hermoth, Hermódr

A Norse messenger god and brother of Balder, Hermod raced directly to the Helheim to rescue his brother following Balder's murder. The condition of Balder's release was that everything in the world must weep for the good god's return. Unfortunately, there were some hold-outs, and Balder stayed dead. Since he had not died in battle, he was not permitted in Valhalla, and was forced to spend his eternity in hell.

⊰ Hoder ⊱
also Hödr, Hodur, Hod, Höd
Norse

The blind god of darkness, Hoder was tricked by the god of mischief (Loki) into killing his brother, Balder, and was subsequently slain by Vali, god of vengeance. Vali was born for the sole purpose of exacting vengeance on Hoder—which he did by growing to an enormous size right after his birth, and then killing the poor, foolish god.

ᕯ LEMMINKÄINEN ᕰ
ALSO LEMMINKAINEN, KAUKO, KAUKO-MIELI, LEMMINKÂINEN

Lemminkäinen is the Finnish trickster god and wizard, mortal enemy of Lempo. Lemminkäinen was chopped to pieces and thrown into the River of the Dead in Tuonela, the Finnish underworld. His grief-struck mother fished out his remains and (with the aid of Suonetar, the Blood goddess) glued them back together using the magical honey belonging to Ukko, the Storm god. This myth bears marked similarity to that of the death of the Egyptian god, Osiris, who was murdered by his brother, dismembered, and dumped in the Nile. Osiris' faithful sister/wife, Isis, collected the pieces and put him back together again, with the help of Anubis and Thoth. Tuonela suffers the same problem as the Helheim of the Norse: it is filled with the lazy, bored, and disenchanted souls of those who never did anything great. Tuonetar (Goddess of the Dead) is queen here, and co-ruler with her husband, Tuoni, god of the dead.

ᕯ LEMPO ᕰ
ALSO JUTAS, JUNTAS, PÄÄPIRU

The Finnish god of evil and misfortune, he is sometimes seen as a triumvirate with the demons Hiisi (who likes to make misfortunes even worse than they originally started) and Paha (evil henchman of Lempo, who also increases misfortune). Paha may be an aspect of Lempo. Lempo is the equivalent of the Christian Satan.

ᕯ LOKI ᕰ
ALSO LOKE, LOKKJU, LOPTI, AND OTHERS
NORSE

Trickster god and general evil-doer of Asgard, Loki is the son of two giants, who schemed his way into being a god of Asgard. One of his many capers involved a giant handyman, who was hired to build a protective wall around Asgard. The giant agreed, on condition that he was given the sun, the moon, and the goddess Frigg as payment. The Asgardians agreed, but stipulated that the job must be completed in one year, which they assumed he could never accomplish.

The giant showed up for work the next day with a wonderous stallion named Svaðilfari ("unlucky traveler"), who could work tirelessly night and day hauling the massive stones for the wall. As the wall neared completion, the Asgardians blamed Loki for getting them into this mess and demanded he do something. Loki changed himself into a sassy mare and lured Svaðilfari away, leaving the giant by himself, unable to finish the wall in time. The giant was enraged and tried to steal Frigg, but Thor crushed the giant's skull with his mighty hammer Mjölnir. Loki, meanwhile, busied himself getting pregnant by Svaðilfari. Loki gave birth to the eight-legged magical stallion Sleipnir ("the sliding one"), which he gifted to Odin (thereby getting himself back into the All Father's good graces).

Loki has a gift for spawning magical offspring. In addition to Sleipnir, he fathered (with a giantess) the terrifying wolf Fenrir; Jörmungandr/Jormungander, the serpent whose length is so great it encircles the earth, waiting with its tail in its mouth for Ragnarök; and Hel/Hela, the demonic goddess of the underworld (the *Helheim*). With a second wife, Loki sired Vali and Narfi. Narfi (also Nörfi, Nörr, Nor, Nari, Narvi, etc.), a nasty god who did bad things, was torn to pieces by his brother Vali when the gods changed Vali into a rabid wolf. Narfi's entrails were used to secure Loki to a massive rock for all eternity—or at least until Ragnarök—as punishment for Loki's murder of Balder. Narfi's brother Vali may or may not be the same Vali who is the god of vengeance who slew Hoder.

⚔ [The] Matres ⚔
also Matronae

These are a Germanic trio of female deities worshipped in northwestern Europe. They are generally believed to have been "mother" goddesses and figures of abundance. The pervasiveness of the "triple goddess" archetype (e.g. the Fates, the Charities, the Maiden-Mother-Crone, etc.) shows how widely dispersed the Celtic peoples were. The Morrígan is herself a triple goddess.

⚔ Nerthus ⚔
also Nerthuz, Hertha, Herta, Hertha

Nerthus is a German fertility goddess who rides in a cart pulled by sacred cows, which are symbols of abundance. She is Mother Nature of the Germans, usually depicted nude with overly abundant assets. A great deal of mystery surrounds her origins and her godhood. She may have been the wife (or a female incarnation) of the ancient sea god, Njord.

⚔ Odin ⚔
also Gangleri, Odinn,
Othinn, Vak, Valtam

Odin is the Norse supreme deity. He is known as Lord of War, Death, and Knowledge, ruler of the other gods (the Æsir) as the "All Father," and mighty king of Asgard, which is the home of the gods.

Odin rides the eight-legged horse Sleipnir, and is accompanied by two wolves and two ravens. The ravens bring continuous updates on the state of affairs from all over the realm of Asgard. Odin has only one eye; he traded the other to Mimir for a drink from the Well of Wisdom near the roots of Yggdrasil, the World Tree. Mimir, formerly a warrior god, exists only as a giant talking head stationed at the Well of Wisdom. Mimir keeps Odin's eye safe, and allows Odin to see into the future.

Legend says that Odin, together with his brothers Ve and Vili/Ville, made the world from the hacked-up body of Ymir, king of the Frost Giants. When they were finished, they banished the remaining Frost Giants to the Jotunheim. Odin is also a shape-shifter (much like Zeus in Greek myth) and loves to travel in various disguises and interact with humans. He is the grandson of the primordial god, Buri (who was born from an ice block licked by the supernatural cow, Audhumla). Odin subsequently fathered most of the rest of the Æsir, including Balder, Hoder, Thor, Vadir, and Hermod.

⊰ SOWILO ⊱
ALSO SIGEL, SUNNE, SOWILŌ, SAEWELŌ

A Germanic god of the sun and Teutonic precursor to the Norse god So, Sowilo's mark looks like this: ⚡, which the Nazis used for the symbol of their secret service. This mark is a common petroglyph, and it stands for the sun (the rays of the sun spreading out).

⊰ THOR ⊱
ALSO THÓRR, THUNOR, DONAR,

Thor is the mighty Norse god of thunder and storms; he rumbles across the sky in a chariot pulled by goats (Tanngniost and Tanngrisnir). He wields the powerful hammer Mjölnir/Mjolnnir, from which great bolts of lightning discharge; the hammer returns to Thor's hand after being thrown, and it is a formidable weapon of war.

Thor is a huge god, bulging with muscle but not with a lot of brains. He is constantly being tricked by Loki into doing all sorts of crazy things, which he never realizes until it's too late. He is married to Sif, goddess of maize/corn with hair of the purest blonde. She suffered horrible embarrassment at the hands of Loki, who snuck into her room one night and cut off all of her beautiful hair. Thor was enraged and threatened to kill Loki, who managed to entreat some talented dwarves to spin Sif a wig from the finest gold thread. (It is curious that Sif became goddess of corn—considering that the grain is a New World native that didn't arrive in the Old World until after the European conquests began.)

With Sif, Thor created a daughter named Thrud, who eventually became one of the Valkyrie (plural also Valkyrie). During an affair with a giantess, he also sired a couple of sons named Magni and Modi. Magni became the god of strength when, at three years old, he freed his trapped father from beneath a dead Stone Giant. Modi (also Móði, Módi, Mothi) became the Norse god of battle and Berserkers, usurping his father's throne as god of those mad fighters. It is commonly thought that Magni and Modi will together inherit Mjölnir following the battle of Ragnarök. Thursday is the weekday named for him.

⊰ TIW ⊱
ALSO TIWAL, TIWAZ, THINGS, ZIU, YEW

Tiw was the Teutonic god of war (German version of the Norse Tyr), and is often associated with Ares (Roman war god). Tiw's name may have been derived from—or may have been applied to—the massive trees that grew abundantly in the British Isles. As a yew tree, he may have been a world tree, or a wooden pillar that held up the sky. Tuesday is named for him.

⊰ TYR ⊱

Tyr was the ancient god of war, reduced to secondary status with the arrival of Odin. Tyr was the original master of the monstrous wolf Fenrir—until Fenrir bit off Tyr's hand when the god was offering it as a sign of trust. Fenrir was then imprisoned in the roots of the world tree, Yggdrasil. Tyr may have been Tuatha Dé Danann, and another aspect of the king Nuada (who also happened to have just one hand). Garm is the hell hound which guards the gates of the *Helheim*. His Greek counterpart is Cerberus, the three-headed dog of Hades. During *Ragnarök*, Garm will break free of his chains but will be killed by Tyr before the final battle. The slaying of Fenrir, however, is the responsibility of Vadir (of the big shoe).

⚔ Vidar ⚖
also Vídarr, Vithar

Norse god of big shoes, Vidar is Odin's son and Thor's brother, whose duty it is to kill the fierce wolf Fenrir after that beast consumes Odin during Ragnarök (Apparently, he is not allowed to kill the wolf *before* it eats the All Father.) Vidar wears a shoe that is made up of all the leftover leather from every shoe ever made; he can stomp any living thing to death while wearing it. He also never speaks, and is called the "Silent God."

⚔ Woden ⚖
also Wōden, Wodan, Wotan, Wodin, Uuôden

Woden was the Anglo-Saxon ruler god (the German version of Odin). His wife was named Frige. Wednesday is the weekday named for him.

Western European Curious Creatures

Norse influences are widely spread through Western Europe and many of these creatures derive from that mythology.

⚔ Gamusino ⚖
Spain

The equivalent of the English "snipe hunt," hunting for the elusive Gamusino is a joke that is played on the naïve or uninitiated members of a group. The novice are sent into the woods with instructions to bring back one of the mysterious creatures. Descriptions are typically wild and conflicting, and practical advice for capturing the creature is usually nonexistent.

⚔ Geri ("greedy") and ⚔ Freki ("ravenous")
Norse

These are the faithful wolf companions of Odin.

⚔ Glas Gaibhnenn ⚔
Norse

Glas (used with various other spellings) is a fabulous cow belonging to the goddess, Boann, which gives unlimited quantities of milk such that the rivers run with it.

⚔ Huldufólk ⚔
Iceland

The invisible fairy folk of Iceland, these are tiny elves, trolls, and fairies who live in the rocks and woods of the island. They don't like civilization, and they are grumpy when disturbed. Custom dictates that the house should be thoroughly cleaned before Christmas Day, and one should leave small offerings of food out for the Huldufólk. On New Year's Day, the creatures migrate as Icelanders light candles to help them find their way in the dark.

⚔ Leprechaun ⚔
Ireland

From the Irish word *lobaircin* ("small-bodied man"), these little men in green are solitary members of the Fey, the fairy folk of Ireland. If you can capture one, he will grant you three wishes in exchange for his freedom. You can catch one by pinning it with your gaze, but don't blink! He will disappear the moment you do. Leprechauns make their living mending shoes—and they are obviously quite good at it, since they are known to have a pot of gold (which you can find *if* you can discover the end of a rainbow).

⚔ Moura Encantada ⚔
Portugal

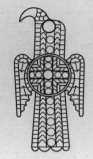

Moura is the enchanted mermaid who will make you rich—if you can break the spell that binds her and set her free. Unfortunately, there are no details that explain who set the curse or how to break it. A Moura can be recognized by her long, beautiful hair and comb of gold.

⚔ Munin/Muninn ⚔
also Hugin/Huginn
Norse

These were the sacred ravens of Odin, ever present on his shoulder. They acted as messengers and spies for the god.

⚔ Nisse ⚔
Denmark

The famous gnomes of Danish mythology, Nisse are dwarflike men who wear conical red caps and live in the lofts of barns. Before the adoption of Julemanden (the Danish Santa Claus), gnomes who were happy with their living arrangements would bring gifts to the children of homeowners on Christmas Day. The little guys have since become famous in the entertainment and advertising industries.

⚔ Saehrímnir ⚔
Norse

Sæhrímnir is a magical animal (generally considered to be a boar) belonging to Odin. It is slaughtered and eaten each night, then reborn again every day.

⚔ Sleipnir ⚔
Norse

Sleipnir is the powerful eight-legged steed of Odin, who helps make the god invincible in battle. Sleipnir is a son of Loki, god of mischief. The horse never tires, and it can transport Odin over land, sea, and through the air. He can even travel to the underworld, Helheim.

⚜ TALLEMAJA ⚜
SWEDEN

Tallemaja is a beautiful troll girl with a tail like a cow. She will try to convince a good man to marry her in a proper Christian church; if she succeeds, she will lose her tail and become human. Unfortunately for her husband, she also loses her beauty.

WESTERN EUROPEAN MYTHICAL MONSTERS

Some of the most iconic monsters in mythology come from Western Europe. Many of these were "acquired" during conquest, and would gain lasting fame via their use as heraldic emblems on coats-of-arms.

⚜ BANSHEE ⚜
ALSO BEAN SÍDHE OR BEAN SÍ
CELTIC, ESPECIALLY IRISH

These wailing announcers of doom and death are the spirits or ghosts of dead women, whose sole purpose is to frighten and disturb the populace. Hearing the cry of a banshee means that death is near.

⚜ BASILISK ⚜
EUROPE, LIKELY GREECE

This is a fearsome chimera usually possessing the head, body, and feet of a rooster, the wings of a bat, and the tail of a snake (sometimes other animal parts are included). Basilisk is said to be born from an egg that was laid by a rooster and incubated by a toad. It is so hideously poisonous that any creature even approaching it will die—including birds flying overhead! Even a look from it can kill. Basilisks are blamed for everything from plague outbreaks to crop failures.

⚔ BLACK SHUCK ⚔
ENGLAND

Black Shuck is a ghost dog that roams the moors of England; it is black-furred and shaggy, with green or red glowing eyes—from which a look can kill, though it might take you a year to die. This legend is likely the inspiration for Conan Doyle's *Hound of the Baskervilles* tale.

⚔ FEAR LIATH ⚔
ALSO AM FEAR LIATH MÒR
SCOTLAND

Essentially a Scottish Big Foot, this creature is said to be 10 feet (3 meters) tall and only reveals its presence by the extreme feeling of dread that it causes when it is nearby. It lives at the top of the second-highest mountain in Scotland, Ben MacDhui.

⚔ FENRIR ⚔
NORSE

The fiercest monster of Norse mythology, Fenrir is a gigantic wolf trapped among the roots of the world tree, Yggdrasil. When Ragnarök comes, Fenrir will escape from the roots and slaughter mankind, as well as eat the All Father, Odin.

⚔ FOMORIANS ⚔
ALSO FOMORACH, FOMOIRE, FOMHÓRAIGH, FOMORII
CELTIC, ESPECIALLY IRISH

These are a race of evil and ugly giants who ruled their conquered peoples through violence and oppression. They demanded exorbitant tribute in the form of two-thirds of all household goods—and two-thirds of all children born. They are the historical enemies of the Tuatha Dé Danann, and were finally defeated by Lugh, who killed their king, Balor.

⚜ GJENGANGER ⚜
NORWAY

These are the ghosts of those who died with unfinished business, who committed suicide, or who were murdered. These spirits are deeply disturbed and cannot rest, committing violence against the living and generally wreaking havoc. They are compared to a poltergeist, a German spirit or ghost that makes noises and moves or tosses things around in rooms. *Poltergeist* is German for "noisy ghost."

⚜ KELPIE ⚜
SCOTLAND

Shaped like a horse, the Kelpie looks benign; it is, however, a deadly water monster that lures its human victims to ride upon its back, then plunges to the depths of the lake or river, where it drowns and eats the hapless person. It can shape-shift to other forms in an attempt to fool its victim. In Ireland, it is called a *phooka* or *pooka*. The Loch Ness Monster is sometimes shown as a kelpie (meaning "water horse" in Scots Gaelic).

⚜ NEBURU ⚜
ASTURIAS/NORTHWEST SPAIN

Neburu (various spellings) is a dark-skinned, dwarvish creature who wears goat skins and a big hat; he drives a chariot pulled by wolves, and he can control the weather—turning it from pleasant to dark and stormy. He is capable of destroying crops, but can also be helpful. He typically has wings and an eye patch.

⚜ OJÁNCANU ⚜
CANTABRIA/SPAIN

Ojáncanu is a pre-Christian monster and a cyclops giant known for his cruelty and ruthless ways. His wife, Ojáncana, is said to be even more brutal than he—she would kill her own children. The Basque people have a similar creature named Tartalo (spelling varies).

⚔ PIRU ⚔
FINLAND

Piru are evil spirits who live in forests and entrap and confuse people who walk through. They are subjects of the devil god, Lempo, and do his bidding.

⚔ TATZELWURM ⚔
BAVARIA

Tatzelwurm was a dragon of the Alps, sometimes described as a medium-sized reptile (about 7–10 feet [2–3 meters] in length) with the head of a cat; wurms generally have just two front legs and no back legs, and stollen can be translated as "stubby feet." It may have poisonous breath, or catlike fangs that can inject venom. It emits catlike yowls, hisses, or growls—or it may whistle. It is considered dangerous to humans.

⚔ TRASGU ⚔
GALICIA/NORTHERN SPAIN

One of any number of "house spirits" (like the Domovoi) that live in human houses, Trasgu (spelling varies) are often mischievous and irascible; they are typically described as tiny men or goblins dressed in red, with red pointy hats (like gnomes from elsewhere). They frequently limp on their spindly legs, and may sport a hole in their left hands. Other descriptions have them wearing brown or black, bearing sheep ears and goat horns. They are generally responsible for various household annoyances such as broken glass, missing or misplaced objects, and creaky stairs. They can be mollified by small offerings of food and thread, and they may even do some household chores at night if they are happy. Getting rid of them means giving them an impossible task (such as turning a black sheep white), then hoping their failure to accomplish it will embarrass them enough that they won't return.

⊰ WOLPERTINGER ⊱
GERMANY

This creature is a chimera made up of various different animal parts, and it is typically fanged and winged. It has a great many similarities with the American Jackalope—particularly its penchant for hanging around taxidermy shops.

WESTERN EUROPEAN SUPERSTITIONS

FRIDAY THE 13TH is a feared date. This isn't unique to Western Europe; many cultures believe that uneven numbers are unlucky, including China, Japan, and the US. What is unique to Western Europe is the specificity of Friday the 13th. The fear is believed to have originated with the fall of the Knights Templar, a highly respected group of former Crusaders known for their righteousness and sense of duty. King Philip IV of France needed money to fund his ambitions, and he knew that the Templars allegedly held vast stores of gold from the Holy Land. He was also deeply in debt to them. On Friday, October 13, 1307, a coordinated mass attack on Templar holdings in France was carried out. The Templars were arrested and all of their goods confiscated. Templars outside of France escaped this fate, but Philip had forced the hand of Pope Clement V, and the Order of the Knights Templar was eventually dissolved.

SAY "BLESS YOU!" when someone sneezes. The relatively dense populations of Western Europe allowed for the scourge of plague to spread fairly easily. Several mass epidemics of the dreaded disease erased huge numbers of people. The worst of all was the Black Death (also the Black Plague), which spread from Asia to Europe in the fall of 1347. By the time it was over, three years later, approximately one-third of the entire population of Europe was dead. The custom of saying "bless you!" to anyone who sneezes is a desperate attempt to invoke the Almighty to stop the spread of disease.

CROSS YOUR FINGERS for luck. This practice may have arisen with the longbow archers of England during the Hundred Years War with France. Allegedly, the bowmen would cross their fingers as they pulled back the bow strings; making the secret "sign of the cross" was believed to help bring God's focus to their aim. The archers devasted the armies of France at the Battle of Crécy in 1346 and at

Agincourt in 1415, in which the French were estimated to have lost eight thousand men to England's one hundred. Ultimately, the French won the war, but the longbow men changed the face of battle forever.

HURTING OR KILLING a cat is bad luck. While many cultures around the world believe that black cats are unlucky, this prohibition against harming *all* cats comes from Germany. The famous Black Forest of Bavaria is home to many witches and assorted unsavory monsters in German folklore. As witches are known to keep cats as familiars, it would not do you good to make the witch angry by hurting her pet. Killing spiders is also considered bad luck, for the same reason.

SEEING AN OLD woman first thing in the morning is bad luck; seeing a young woman is good luck. The Germans have a great number of admonitions concerning old women, many of which have the reverse effect if a young woman is involved. Again, witches.

AN ITCHY PALM means money will come to you soon. This superstition actually spread from African slaves. A Nigerian belief says that an itchy right palm means you will receive money, while an itchy left palm means you will lose money.

DON'T WALK UNDER an open ladder. This superstition has an interesting source. It seems that the open ladder forms a triangle—a shape known to be especially magical. Walking under the ladder breaks the mystical shape (and perhaps upsets the various spirits living there), disturbing the symmetry and bringing bad luck. In some traditions, it can even kill you.

BREAKING A MIRROR is seven years' bad luck. Not only are mirrors extremely expensive historically, but some cultures believe that the mirror actually captures the soul of the viewer. Breaking the mirror kills the soul, and the viewer will inevitably die. This same belief still exists in the dislike of being photographed that is prevalent in some cultures. The reason for it being seven years is that this has long been a magical number in many traditions—including Christianity.

A HORSESHOE IS good luck. Horses are extremely important to nomadic peoples across the world. Owning a horse is often a sign of wealth, and possessing anything associated with—or showing a

picture of—a horse increased your chances of gaining wealth. Be sure to hang your horseshoe over the front door with the ends facing up. Doing so keeps the good luck from draining out of the horseshoe.

SWIMMING IN FREEZING cold water on the first day of the New Year brings good health for the entire year. This belief has since morphed into a worldwide phenomenon of "polar bear plunging." Rather than being for health benefits, the current fad is more about how cold the water is and how long the swimmers can stay in it (the Netherlands).

CARRYING THE BRIDE over the threshold is good luck. This ancient superstition stems from the belief in house spirits: if the bride were to stumble while entering her new home, evil spirits could catch her unprepared and enter her body, causing difficult childbirths or even sterility. Carrying the bride through this dangerous passage avoids this.

IF A VIRGIN wants to know whether she'll marry in the coming year, she should knock on a chicken coop at midnight on Christmas Eve. If a rooster squawks, she will marry; if a hen squawks, she won't (Germany).

IF A YOUNG woman walks backwards into a garden on Midsummer's Eve (the Summer Solstice) and picks a rose, she can discover who she will marry. The rose must be carefully placed into a paper bag and stored in a dark drawer until Christmas Eve. On Christmas Day, the rose is removed from the bag and worn in the décolletage to church. The man who asks for the rose (or who takes it without asking) will be her future groom (England).

TO PREVENT GOBLINS from substituting changelings for your child, lay a pair of men's pants over the cradle (Germany).

THE CORPSE OF a murdered person will bleed if it is touched by the person who killed it. In times past, touching the corpse was a way of proving guilt—or innocence—of having committed the murder. Thankfully, this trial is no longer practiced (England).

Australia and Oceania

There is incredible variety in the independent nations of the Pacific Ocean. Modern Australian tradition derives from its roots as a European penal colony, but the vast number of aboriginal tribes and the unique geographical attributes of the continent have exerted their influence as well. Pacific island nations were settled by various ethnic and political groups; while many of them share somewhat similar mythical and religious roots, others have developed beliefs that are unique to them alone. The enormous expanse of the ocean provided a real barrier to homogenization and allowed for the development of some truly interesting practices and beliefs.

Australia is the world's smallest and flattest continent and is the only nation that governs an entire continent—which happens to be the driest continent on earth. The Outback (the largely unpopulated interior of the country) receives about 11 inches of rain a year, which isn't a lot, but it greatly exceeds the less than one inch that falls in the driest part of the Sahara. The term *Oceania* refers to the entire body of islands—including Australia—throughout the South and Central Pacific Ocean. The area of the Pacific Ocean is larger than the area of all of the earth's landmasses *combined*. There are thousands of islands scattered across the Pacific, which can generally be lumped into three broad categories: continental islands (including Australia, New Zealand, and New Guinea), high islands (also "volcanic" islands such as those in Melanesia, and the "Ring of Fire" area of the Pacific), and low islands (such as those of Micronesia and Polynesia—including the Hawaiian Islands). These different types of island groups are based on how they formed geologically, a topic well beyond the scope of this book.

The mythology of Oceania is a polyglot of varying gods, legends, and traditions far too numerous to recount here (even Australia has over nine hundred different aboriginal tribes). Many of the beliefs are similar, differing mostly in the details. Others are vastly different, and their origins are shrouded in mystery (Easter Island). Here's a look at some of the mythology of this incredibly rich and varied region.

AUSTRALIAN GODS AND GODDESSES

Most of these derive from aboriginal tribes that have lived in the region for thousands of years. The Dreamtime is a mythical period of time when gods and goddesses created and roamed the earth.

⊰ ADNO-ARTINA ⊱

He is the Diyari spirit guardian of Uluru (Ayers Rock), who inhabits the form of a lizard.

⊰ ALTJIRA ⊱
ALSO LTJIRA MARA, ALCHERA

Creator god of the Aranda people, Altjira created the world and everything in it—then disappeared without any more contact.

⊰ BAIAME ⊱
ALSO BIAME

Sky god of the Kamilaroi people and the creator and teacher of man, Baiame made the world and everything in it. He taught humans the skills of hunting, fishing, and predicting the weather—plus many other things.

⊰ BIRRAHGNOOLOO ⊱

Birrahgnooloo is the fertility goddess of the Kamilaroi people and wife of Baiame and mother of Daramulum.

⚜ DARAMULUM ⚜
ALSO NURUNDERE, PAPANG

Daramulum is the All Father and sky god of the Kamilaroi, and the son of Baiame and Birrahgnooloo, the Supreme Creators. He lives in the moon, from which he watches the goings-on of earth, creates the weather, and protects shamans. He only has one leg.

⚜ EINGANA ⚜
ALSO EINGANU

Eingana is the Dreamtime snake goddess who gave birth to humanity, as well as all of the marine animals of the world. She helps the Wandjina straighten out the humans of the world.

⚜ LUMALUMA ⚜

God of gluttony, Lumaluma began as a whale in the sea who came to land to exchange his knowledge for food—lots of food. He took to showing up at feasts (invited or not) and eating everything in sight. His hunger grew until he took to eating dead children. The people could not abide that, so they rose up against him and tried to kill him and his wives. This took a long time, partly because Lumaluma was the size of a whale, and partly because he demanded that his death be performed according to certain rituals. The people tired of this and tied his mangled body to a tree. They built a shade hut over it and left it to rot. Eventually, the body disappeared. Some believe scavengers ate it; some believed that Lumaluma turned back into a whale and escaped to the sea.

⚜ MOKOI ⚜
ALSO MOKPOI

Evil spirit of the Yolngu people, Mokoi can be invoked by dark shamans using black magic, and will do their bidding. Shamans beware! If you lose control over Mokoi, he will dispose of you in a terrible fashion.

⚜ [THE] RAINBOW SNAKE ⚜
ALSO ALMUDJ, KALSERU

The Rainbow Snake is a fertility goddess and mother of humanity, as well as goddess of plant growth and the cooling rain. The Snake is a chimera with the head of a kangaroo, the tail of a crocodile, and the body of a python. She is decorated all over with water lilies and waving tendrils of green growth. Yingarna is the female aspect of the Snake, the Mother of Creation. Her son is Ngalyod, the male aspect of the Snake, the Great Transformer of the Land. Cave paintings and petroglyphs have illustrations of the Rainbow Snake dating back over eight thousand years ago—making this deity one of the oldest on earth.

⚜ WALAGANDA ⚜
ALSO WALANGANDA, WALLUNGUNDER

Walaganda is the chief god of the Wandjina. He descended from the Milky Way during the Dreamtime and made the earth and all living things. Having finished this task, he was less than pleased with the results. He went back home, then returned to earth again, this time bringing the Wandjina with him. With Eingana's help, they birthed the humans, then spent a considerable part of the Dreamtime teaching the beings they had created how to be people.

⊰ WANDJINA ⊱
ALSO WONDJINA

These are spirits of the Dreamtime that are powerful beings with no mouths, but enormous eyes sunk in oversized heads, atop bodies with very long arms and legs. Yes, they looked like space aliens, and this recollection is backed by ancient cave art discovered in the early nineteenth century. The Wandjina descended from space (the Milky Way, to be precise), giving learning, law, and civilization to the people.

⊰ YHI ⊱

A "dreamy" creation goddess, Yhi woke during the Dreamtime and saw that all around her was barren. Her waking brought light to the darkness; as she walked across the land, flowers and trees grew in her footsteps. As she looked into caves and valleys, butterflies and beautiful insects fluttered forth. In the shadowy places, she felt spirits yearning for freedom. She gave them bodies, and all the creatures of the land sprang from the dark places. Pleased with her efforts, Yhi departed.

Unfortunately, her skills as a builder left something to be desired. Most of her animals had no legs or wings, nor any way to move about. The creatures of the world prayed to her, and they bid her to return—which she did. She gave all the creatures their moving parts, but many of these were odd: a duck's bill and feet on an animal with fur; a deep pocket on a giant hopping rabbit; several birds with wings that couldn't fly but instead ran about on big feet; a bear with legs too short to walk on, which instead was stuck in the trees eating leaves.

Yhi saw a naked animal that walked about on two spindly legs, "Did I make that?" she wondered. She saw that the animal was lonely and she offered to make it a mate. The animal had some fear about what the goddess would make for him, but she created the perfect mate: she created woman, and the animal became a man, and they were happy on the earth. Then Yhi returned to the Dreamtime for good.

Oceanic Gods and Goddesses

The gods and goddesses of Oceania vary greatly due to the isolating effects of island living.

⊰ Adi-Mailagu ⊱
Fiji

Goddess of the sky, she comes to earth in the form of a gray rat, but can shape-shift into a beautiful woman—or a horrible hag with a yard-long tongue. If a man makes love to her beautiful self, he will die.

⊰ Hina ⊱
Tahiti

Hina is the moon goddess and goddess of creativity and feminine power. She is also mother to the god Oro. To the Maori, she is Hine, goddess of the night-time and death. In her aspect as Hine-Keha, she is the full moon; as Hine-Uri, she is the Purple Lady, goddess of the new moon. As Hine-Titama, she is goddess of the dawn, maiden of the light—until she learned that her beloved husband, Táne, is also her father. The knowledge shatters her, and she flees to the underworld and refuses to return. Táne changs her name to Hine-Nui-Te-Po, goddess of death and lady of the night. She looks after the dead in the underworld.

⊰ Kane ⊱
Hawai'i

God of procreation and the sea, he is part of the trinity of creator gods, along with Ku and Lono. He is associated with the Maori Táne.

≈ Ku ≈
ALSO KU-KA-PUA, KU-KUA-ALSOHI
HAWAI'I

A hideously ugly god of war, Ku is the head of the creator trinity with Kane and Lono.

≈ Lono ≈
HAWAI'I

Lono is the popular god of food, music, and fertility and the third member of the creator god trinity with Ku and Kane. Offerings of songs and sweet potatoes make him happy, and he brings the soft rains. Lono's twin brother, Kanaloa, is god of the underworld.

≈ Maui ≈
ALSO MAUI-TIKITIKI-A-TARANGA
NEW ZEALAND

A Maori trickster god, Maui was born as a jellyfish and thrown into the sea by his mother. Tama-nui-te-ra, the sun god, rescued him and dried him out so that he looked like a proper boy, then returned him to his mother. His father, god of the underworld, gave him a magic fish hook that could catch anything. Maui showed off by pulling up some fish so big that they became islands. He also hooked the sun and slowed its movements. He came to an untimely end when he tried to fool around with the enormous goddess, Hine-nui-te-po, without her consent. She squashed him between her gigantic legs.

≈ Nangananga ≈
FIJI

Goddess of death, she guards the gates of Heaven—where only married men may enter.

⚄ NDAUTHINA ⚄
FIJI

God of fire, he lights the night to aid sailors in navigation.

⚄ ORO ⚄
TAHITI

A war god, Oro fights with a spear, and has three daughters who drive him mad: Toi-mata, "axe eye," Ai-tupuai, "head eater," and Mahu-fatu-rau, "escape from a hundred stones." The girls loved to push their father's buttons, while the god's son Hoa-Tapu, "faithful friend," seems to be his father's favorite.

⚄ PELE ⚄
HAWAI'I

Pele is a volcano goddess who makes her home in the active volcano Kilauea.

⚄ RIGI ⚄
NAURU

Rigi was a white worm that gave its life to create the Milky Way. Before that, its sweat made the seas of the world.

⚄ TA'AROA ⚄
TAHITI

Ta'aroa is the feathered creator god of the universe. There were two eggs in the beginning, and Ta'aroa was born from one of them. When he hatched, he cooked his own flesh and made the land. He created mountains from his stewed bones, and clouds from the steam of his boiling organs. He rolled his intestines into eels, and squeezed his blood to make birds. All manner of flowers were made from his feathers. The sun was made from the egg yolk, and the moon and stars from leftover pieces of eggshell. Together with Hina, he fathered the god Oro.

Australian and Oceanic Mythical Monsters

There are multiple ethnicities in this section, including Japanese and Southeast Asian.

⊰ Abaia ⊱
New Guinea/Melanesia

A giant eel monster that lives at the bottom of freshwater lakes, Abaia protects fish and animals in the lake as if they are its children. Anyone trying to catch a fish or lake animal will be swept away by a huge wave from the Abaia's tail.

⊰ Bunyip ⊱
Australia

An aboriginal monster of the wet places of Australia, it has several features, which usually include dark fur and nasty, pointy teeth.

⊰ Drop Bear ⊱
Australia

These are giant koalas that like to fall out of trees and eat tourists with their sharp teeth. These are "joke" creatures, like snipes and Gamusinos, whose stories are told to the naïve to make them look foolish.

⊰ Moehau ⊱
also Maero, Matau,
Tuuhourangi, Taongina, Rapuwai
New Zealand

Moehau is a man-sized ape-like creatures, with long shaggy hair and very long fingers with sharp nails or claws. They are believed to eat people, and have been blamed for some documented deaths.

⊰ Nanaue ⊱
Hawai'i

Nanaue is a shark-man, resulting from the mating of the shark king, Kamohoalii, and a human woman. The Nanaue can shape-shift between a normal man and a shark-man. When in normal-man form, he has a huge gaping shark mouth on his back; when in shark-man form, his hunger is uncontrollable. He kills many people before the Molokai people finally kill him.

⊰ Ningen ⊱
Antarctica and surrounding islands

From the Japanese for "human," these large-bodied, white-skinned monsters can reach lengths of 100 feet (30 meters). They have human-like eyes and mouths, along with fins or flippered hands and feet. Some believe that Ningen sightings are really beluga whales.

⊰ Taniwha ⊱
New Zealand/Polynesia

A very large sea serpent of fresh or salt water, Taniwha may be able to shape-shift to dragon, whale, or shark forms. It is definitely man-eating.

⊰ Yara-ma-yha-who ⊱
Australia

An aboriginal vampire, it is described as a short red thing that resembles a demon. It has no teeth, but drops out of trees onto its victims and sucks their blood with octopus-style suckers on its hands and feet. If it decides to eat a victim, it will then sleep and vomit the person back up after it wakes. The person may or may not still be alive.

⊰ Yowie ⊱
also quinkin, joogabinna
Australia

The "down-under" version of Bigfoot, Yowie are humanoids standing over 6 feet (1.9 meters) tall, with flattened noses and dark brown or black fur.

Australian and Oceanic Superstitions

Again, as a result of cultural mixing, the superstitions of this region are quite different from those found elsewhere.

Killing a willy-wagtail bird makes the bird's spirit angry; it can cause outbreaks of violence that kill people (Australia).

Don't put a shoe on the dinner table. If you do, someone close to you will die (Australia).

Don't whistle in graveyards, a ghost might follow you home (Australia).

Don't cut finger or toenails at night, you'll summon demons (Malaysia).

THE "MIN MIN lights" (unexplained atmospheric phenomena) are the spirits of dead ancestors who watch over you. Others believe that the lights try to distract you from your chosen path. They can even come down and carry you away if you stare at them too long (Australia/New Zealand).

IF YOU GET lost at night, take your shirt off, turn it inside out, and then put it on that way. You will find your way home (Philippines).

TOUCH (OR TAKE A PINCH OF) food that you didn't get to eat in order to avoid *kempunan* (cravings). Kempunan that go unsatisfied can lead to death and a soul that is unable to rest (Malaysia).

DON'T GO TO bed with wet hair or you will go blind (Philippines).

WHEN A CHILD loses a tooth, they must throw it up on the roof so that the new tooth will grow in straight (Philippines).

DURING A STORM, cover the mirrors with black cloth so that lightning can't enter the house (Australia).

DON'T LIGHT THREE cigarettes off a single match. This is a superstition believed by soldiers in most countries. You see, a sniper *sees* the first, *aims* with the second, and *fires* at the third. Don't be that third guy (Australia, and elsewhere).

IF A WOMEN blows a digeridoo, she will become pregnant (aboriginal Australia).

About the Author

D.R. McElroy is a professional writer and editor. She has written two previous books and a host of articles for various publications. Ms. McElroy possesses a Bachelor of Science in Horticulture and an Master of Science in Environmental Resources. She is hard at work on her next book. D.R. McElroy can be reached at her website DebraMcElroy.com

Acknowledgments

My first acknowledgement is my dear husband, Kevin, who puts up with my late-night writing and late-morning/noon-ish risings every day. I need to thank my brother, Pat, for his continued belief in my writing skills, even when I wasn't sure of that myself at one point. I also want to thank my editor, John Foster, at Quarto Publishing, for his kindness and patience when I get my artistic neck hairs up, and all of the people whose behind the scenes work makes these books so beautiful.

Photo Credits

Unless otherwise listed below, all images © Shutterstock

© Alamy
Page 25: Gilgamesh; Science History Images
Page 46: Hanuman worshipping Rama, who sits with his wife Sita and her brother Lakshman; Science History Images
Page 78: Killer whale; Patrick Guenette
Page 79: Wolf; Quagga Media
Page 86: Hopi Crow Mother katchina doll; John Cancalosi

© Bridgeman Images
Page 68: Koloowisi (plumed serpent); Look and Learn / Elgar Collection
Page 177: Rainbow snake; Dreamtime Gallery, London

Courtesy of WikiMedia Commons
Page 134: *Perperuna's Dance* by Marek Hapon

INDEX

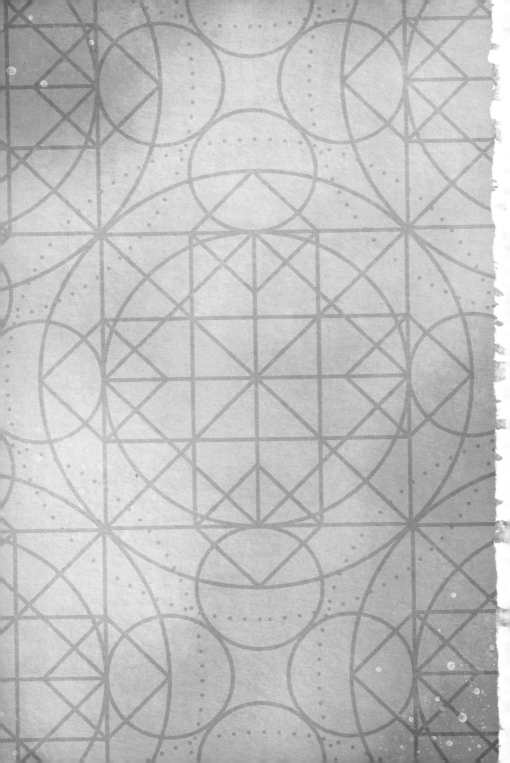